I0131385

# Family Tax Benefits for Qualifying Child and Qualifying Relative Dependents

# For 2017 Tax Returns

## James M. Hopkins, CPA

**To my wife, Cheryl, and family for the encouragement to complete this project. JMH**

Text © 2017 by James M. Hopkins, CPA
All rights reserved. No part of this book may be reproduced or transmitted in any form or by any means, electronic or mechanical, including photocopying, recording, or by any information storage and retrieval system, without permission of the publisher.

ISBN (softbound): 978-0-9985233-2-3
ISBN (e-book): 978-0-9985233-3-0

The author is responsible for the contents of this book. Please email any comments you have about the contents to the author.

**Author's Background**
James Hopkins is an adjunct faculty member at Morningside College in Sioux City, IA. He worked in public accounting for seven years, private industry for six years, and was a full-time faculty member at Morningside College teaching all accounting classes for thirty years. He recently retired as a full-time professor, now teaching one class a semester and has a tax consulting practice in the Sioux City area. Feel free to contact him at **hopkins@morningside.edu**.

**Disclaimer of warranty**

This book is written to provide accurate and authoritative information regarding the subject matter covered. The book is sold with the understanding the author is not engaged in rendering tax preparation or tax planning services. It is intended as a guide to the topics covered. Readers needing tax preparation and or tax planning assistance should retain the services of a qualified professional of their choice.

# Family Tax Benefits for Qualifying Children and Qualifying Relatives

## Table of Contents

## Chapter 1

## Overview

The income tax law provides several income tax benefits for taxpayers and their dependents.

These include:

- Personal and dependency exemptions,
- Qualifying children (QC) dependents,
- Qualifying relative (QR) dependents,
- Child tax credit (CTC),
- Child and dependent care credit,
- Income exclusion for dependent care benefits,
- Earned income tax credit (EITC or EIC), and
- Head of household filing status (abandoned spouse).

Each will be discussed in a separate chapter.

## Recent Update

The Internal Revenue Service issued proposed regulations (IRS-REG-137604-07) on January 19, 2017; Fed Reg. Vol. 82, No. 12, p. 6370, or Internal Revenue Bulletin No. 2017-7, dated February 13, 2017, pages 920-940.

That document contains proposed amendments to Internal Code Sections 2, 3, 21, 32, 63, 151, 152, 6013, and 6109 reflecting changes made by Working Families Tax Reform Act of 2004 (WFTRA, Pub. L. 108-311, 118 Stat. 1166, 1169, enacted in October

2004) and the Fostering Connections to Success and Increasing Adoptions Act (FCSIAA, Pub. L. 110-351, 122 Stat. 3949, enacted in October 2008).

WFTRA amended Sec. 152 to provide a uniform definition of a qualifying child. FCSIAA expanded the qualifying child definition the requirements that the child must be younger than the claiming taxpayer and that the child must not file a joint return other than as a claim for refund

The proposed regulations update existing regulations pertaining to surviving spouse, head of household filing status, individuals' use of tax tables, dependent care expenses, earned income credit, defining taxable income (Sec. 63), definition of a dependent, joint returns, and use of identifying numbers.

The regulations would apply to tax years beginning after the date they are published as final regulations. Pending the issuance as final regulations, taxpayers can choose to *apply the proposed regulations in any open tax* years.

When finalized, the proposed regulations will obsolete Rev. Rul. 57-344, Rev. Rul. 58-67, Rev. Rul. 58-302, Rev. Rul. 64-223, Rev. Rul. 65-307, Rev. Rul. 70-341, Rev. Rul. 74-153, Rev. Rul. 74-543, Rev. Rul. 79-173, Rev. Rul. 84-89, Notice 2006-86, and Notice 2008-5. Guidance in these directives has been incorporated into the proposed regulations or is no longer relevant.

Summaries of the proposed changes are shown at the end of each chapter within the book. A complete copy of the proposed regulations is included at the end of this book.

## Chapter 2

## Personal Exemptions

## In General

A personal exemption ($3,950 for 2014; $4,000 for 2015; $4,050 for 2016 and 2017) is allowed an individual taxpayer when electing single filing status. Married taxpayers filing married filing jointly (MFJ) are each allowed a personal exemption.[1] In general, no other person is entitled to an exemption for either spouse when a joint return is filed, even though a spouse would be entitled to an exemption for one of the spouses as a dependent if a joint return was not filed.[2]

A married taxpayer filing a separate return can take one personal exemption deduction and a personal exemption for a spouse, if the spouse for the calendar year in which the married taxpayer's year begins (1) has no gross income, (2) is not a dependent of another taxpayer, and (3) is not filing a tax return.[3]

Exceptions to rules exist in many tax situations, and one exists to allow someone else (a parent) to claim a child, even when the child is married and files a joint

---

[1] See IRS Pub 17 (2016), p 25.

[2] Reg. Sec. 1.151-1(b).

[3] IRC Sec. 151(b).

15

return with his or her spouse. If the child's joint return is filed to claim a refund and no tax would be shown for either spouse on separate returns, or on a joint return, then another person may claim an exemption for one of the spouses provided all other conditions for a dependency exemption are satisfied.[4]

A spouse is not considered a dependent of the other spouse.[5] Exemption amounts are adjusted annually for changes in the consumer price index.[6]

> **Example 2-1:** Jane is filing a separate return for the 2016 year. She is entitled to a $4,050 exemption on her personal tax return. If Jane was married, she and her spouse could file as MFJ and have total exemptions of $8,100. The considerations of dependent children, subject to many different requirements, will be discussed later.

A taxpayer, who qualifies as a dependent of another taxpayer,    is denied a personal exemption.[7]    This

---

[4] IRC Sec. 152(b)(2); Rev. Rul. 54-567, 1954-2 CB 108; Rev. Rul.65-34, 1965-1, CB 86.

[5] Ibid. Pub 17, p 25.

[6] IRC Sec. 151(d)(4).

[7] IRC Sec. 151 (d)(2), enacted by the Tax Reform Act of 1986, P.L. 99-517 effective for years beginning in 1987. Prior to 1987, a dependent and the other taxpayer were each allowed an exemption amount. Parents claiming a

prevents the dependent taxpayer and the other taxpayer from each claiming an exemption (two in total) for the same individual.

> **Example 2-2:** If Jane is not married, but could be claimed on her parents' tax return as their dependent, Jane will not have a personal exemption claimed on her personal return.[8]

> **Example 2-3:** If Jane was married during the current tax year and files a joint return with her spouse, her parents cannot claim her exemption even if all other qualifying child dependency conditions are satisfied. However, if a joint return was filed to claim a refund and no tax is shown on a joint return and on Jane and her spouse's separate returns, then Jane's parents can claim an exemption for her.[9]

> **Planning Pointer:** In this situation, Example 2-3, consideration should be

---

child as a dependent and the dependent on his or her return each got an exemption.

[8] Jane is denied a personal exemption even if her parents fail to claim her as a dependent. See Chief Counsel Advice 200236001.

[9] IRS Pub 501 (2016), p 13; Rev. Rul. 54-567, 1954-2 CB 108; Rev. Rul. 65-34, 1965-1 CB 86.

given to the benefits of having Jane and her spouse file as married filing separately (MFS) or married filing jointly (MFJ) to determine which is more advantageous before any returns are filed. Married taxpayers filing as MFS can amend their returns and file as MFJ; however, a MFJ return cannot be amended to file MFS returns.[10]

## Married Taxpayers Filing Separate Returns

As previously mentioned, a taxpayer filing married filing separately (MFS) can claim a personal exemption for a spouse on a separate return, provided the other spouse has no gross income and is not a dependent of any other taxpayer.[11]

The test for not being a dependent of any other taxpayer and the no gross income test are based on the calendar year in which the taxable year of the taxpayer claiming the spouse's exemption begins.[12] If the taxpayer claiming the spouse's exemption and the spouse have the same calendar year, then the spouse being claimed must have no gross income for the entire calendar, taxable year and may not be a dependent of any other taxpayer for that calendar year.

---

[10] IRC Sec. 6013(b)(2) and Reg. Sec. 1.6013-1(a).

[11] IRC Sec. 151(b).

[12] Reg. Sec. 1.151-1(b).

If the taxpayer claiming the spouse's exemption has a fiscal year that is not a calendar year, the spouse being claimed must have no gross income and not be the dependent of any other taxpayer for the entire calendar year in which the claiming spouse's fiscal year begins.

> **Example 2-4:** If the spouse claiming a spouse's exemption on a MFS return has a fiscal year beginning on August 1 and ends on July 31, then the spouse being claimed must have no gross income and not be a dependent of any other taxpayer for the entire calendar year of the claiming spouse, which is January 1 to December 31. This period starts seven months before the start of the claiming spouse's fiscal year of August 1.[13]

No gross income means any gross income. A spouse who has gross income in this situation that does not require a return be filed cannot be claimed by the other spouse. [14]

In a situation where married taxpayers each have gross income, each filed as MFS, and claimed their spouse as a personal exemption, the Tax Court disallowed the husband's personal exemption for his spouse, but the

---

[13] IRC Sec. 151(b).

[14] Id.

issue of the wife's personal exemption for her husband was not addressed by the court.[15]

## Additional Personal Exemptions for Age 65 and Over and Blind

Additional personal exemptions were available to individuals and spouses if they were age 65 or over or blind before the close of the tax year. This provision was repealed effective for tax years beginning after December 31, 1986.[16]

Taxpayers age 65 or over, or blind, receive an additional, limited standard deduction amount.[17] A taxpayer satisfying both conditions is entitled to two additional, limited standard deductions. [18]

These two additional, limited standard deductions are available only if the taxpayers use the standard deduction, and are lost if they itemize personal deductions.

---

[15] *Dillion, Sam,* TCM 1993-19, aff'd., without published opinion, (5th Cir 1993) 73 AFTR 2d, 94-781, 14 F3d 52.

[16] Tax Reform Act of 1986 (P.L. 99-514 Sec. 103(b), amending IRC Sec. 151).

[17] IRC Sec. 63(f)(1).

[18] IRC Sec. 63 (c)(3).

## Personal Exemptions for Resident and Nonresident Aliens

Resident aliens are allowed a personal exemption subject to the same rules as a U.S. citizen.[19] Nonresident aliens are allowed a personal exemption on income effectively connected to a U.S. trade or business.[20] A personal exemption is not allowed to a non-resident alien on income not effectively connected to a U.S. trade or business.[21]

## Personal Exemptions and Short Tax Years

When a change in accounting period creates a short tax year requiring the general method of income annualization, each full exemption amount must be reduced. Each month in the short tax year is allowed 1/12th of the total exemption amount.[22]

## Personal Exemptions in the Year of Death

A surviving spouse is allowed a full personal exemption in the year of death for a deceased spouse on a MFJ return with the deceased spouse.[23] A taxpayer filing as MFS for the year when his or her spouse died can claim a personal exemption for the deceased

---

[19] IRS Pub. 519 (2016), p 27.

[20] Id.

[21] IRC Sec. 873(a).

[22] IRC Sec. 443(b) and (c).

[23] IRS Pub 17 (2016), p 25.

spouse provided the three tests for a living spouse, previously discussed are satisfied.[24]

A surviving spouse who remarries in the year of death of the first spouse cannot claim a personal exemption for the first spouse because the surviving spouse is married to a new spouse and exemptions are determined at the end of the year.[25]

Also, a surviving spouse who remarries in the year of death of the first spouse cannot claim the first spouse as a qualifying relative for a dependency exemption. A deceased spouse is not a qualifying relative, so a surviving taxpayer cannot claim a dependency exemption for a deceased spouse.[26]

A surviving spouse who has no gross income, and is not a dependent of an another taxpayer who remarries in the year of death, can be claimed as an exemption on the deceased spouse's final separate return and on the separate return of the new spouse. Note both of these must be separate returns.[27]

A surviving spouse, who has no gross income and is not a dependent of another taxpayer who remarries in

---

[24] Id.

[25] Rev. Rul. 71-158, 1971-1 CB 50.

[26] IRC Sec. 152(d)(2)(H).

[27] IRS Pub 17 (2016), p 25.

the year of death and files MFJ with second spouse, has only one exemption.[28]

If a surviving spouse obtained a final divorce decree or separate maintenance before the end of the year, the surviving spouse cannot claim a former spouse's exemption, even if the surviving spouse provided all of the former spouse's support.[29]

All personal and dependency exemptions require a taxpayer identification number be shown on the tax return claiming the exemption.[30]

## Phase-out of Personal and Dependency Exemptions

The personal and dependency (discussed later) exemption amounts are reduced by 2% for each $2,500 (or fraction thereof) the taxpayers' Adjusted Gross Income (AGI) exceeds the taxpayers' AGI threshold amount. For married filing separately, the reduction is 2% for each $1,250 that the AGI exceeds the taxpayers' threshold AGI amount.

---

[28] Id.

[29] Id.

[30] IRC Sec. 151(e).

The 2016 threshold amounts for each filing status are presented in the following table:

| Filing Status | Phase-out Start | Phase-out Completed |
|---|---|---|
| Married filing jointly and surviving spouse (QW) | $311,300 | $433,800 |
| Single | $259,400 | $381,900 |
| Head of household | $285,350 | $407,850 |
| Married filing separately | $155,650 | $216,900 |

The 2017 threshold amounts for each filing status are presented in the following table:

| Filing Status | Phase-out Start | Phase-out Completed |
|---|---|---|
| Married filing jointly and surviving spouse (QW) | $313,800 | $436,300 |
| Single | $261,500 | $384,000 |
| Head of household | $287,650 | $410,150 |
| Married filing separately | $156,900 | $218,150 |

## Effect of Proposed Regulations

The proposed regulations remove the provisions related to an additional exemption for age and blindness under Sec. 151 and adds regulations under Sec. 63 for additional standard deduction for age and blindness to reflect changes by the Tax Reform Act of 1986. Each spouse who has attained age 65 before the end of the taxable year is entitled to an additional standard deduction on a joint return.

A married taxpayer who files a separate return is entitled to additional amount for the taxpayer's spouse if the spouse has attained age 65 before the end of the taxable year and, for the calendar year in which the

24

taxable year of the taxpayer begins, the spouse has no gross income and is not the dependent of another taxpayer.

A taxpayer is not entitled to an additional standard deduction amount if the spouse dies before reaching age 65, even though the spouse would have attained age 65 before the end of the taxpayer's year end.

Taxpayers claiming a tax benefit for blindness do not have to attach certificate or statement to their return for such benefit.    Instead, they must maintain such information in their files.

## Chapter 3

## Dependency Exemption Requirements for Qualifying Children and Qualifying Relatives

The tax law provides for two categories of dependency exemptions (1) qualifying child or (2) qualifying relative created effective with years starting in 2005 by the Working Families Tax Relief Act, Public Law 108-311 enacted in 2004, amending Sec. 152 in its entirety. The specifics for each category will be discussed in detail in later chapters. This chapter will discuss the three dependency exemption requirements for both qualifying child and qualifying relative categories. These three requirements are: (1) dependent taxpayer test; (2) joint return test; and (3) citizenship or residency test.

## Dependents of another Taxpayer

A person claimed as a dependent by another taxpayer for any taxable year of another person is denied a personal exemption on his or her own tax return and cannot have any dependents on his or her personal return for the taxable year that begins in the calendar year of the other taxpayer.[31] This rule applies even if the dependent's exemption is not claimed on another

---

[31] IRC Sec. 152(b)(1).

taxpayer's return or if the exemption is lost due to high adjusted gross income phase out.[32]

> **Example 3-1:** Jane is a full-time college student and is claimed as a dependent on her parents' personal income tax return. She is denied her personal exemption on her personal return, as previously discussed. She also cannot declare dependents on her personal return for any children, if all other requirements for a dependency exemption are satisfied. If her parents claim her on their 2016 calendar year return, Jane cannot have her personal exemption or any dependent children exemptions on her 2016 return. Any benefits for Jane's children such as earned income credit, dependency exemptions, child tax credit, child and dependent care credit, child and dependent care benefits could be shifted to her parents provided they satisfy all requirements with respect to Jane's children.
>
> **Planning Pointer:** The dependent child and parents will most likely have tax years that coincide, which makes

---

[32] Chief Counsel Advice 200236001.

application of this rule easier. When the parents' and dependent child's tax years coincide, the dependent child's tax return for the same tax year as the parents cannot claim any personal or dependency exemptions. If they have different taxable years, this provision prevents the dependent child or any potential dependent claimed on another taxpayer's return from having any dependents for the dependent's taxable year beginning in the same taxable year as the taxable year of the taxpayer claiming the dependency exemption.[33] The following examples illustrate applications of this rule.

**Example 3-2:** Assume the parents have a taxable, calendar year of January 1, 2011 to December 31, 2011, while the dependent had a July 1, 2011 to June 30, 2012 fiscal tax year. The application of this rule prevents the dependent from having any personal or dependency exemptions for the tax year, July 2011 to June 2012, since that tax year begins in the calendar year, January 1, 2011 to December 31, 2011, where the dependent is claimed as an exemption.

---

[33] IRC Sec. 152 (b)(1).

**Example 3-3:** Assume a reversal of the facts in the prior example. The parents have a taxable year of July 1, 2011 to June 30, 2012 while their dependent has a calendar year, taxable year of January 1, 2011 to December 31, 2011. The application of this rule prevents the dependent from having any personal or dependency exemptions for the calendar taxable year of January 1, 2012 to December 31, 2012, as the dependent's taxable, calendar year starting January 1, 2012 begins in the July 1, 2011 to June 30, 2012 fiscal year of the taxpayers claiming her dependency exemption.

**Dependents Filing Joint Returns**

In general, qualifying child and qualifying relative dependents who file a joint return with a spouse cannot be claimed as dependent by another taxpayer unless the filing of the joint return was to obtain a refund and no income tax would be shown on the MFJ return and on married filing separate returns of each spouse.[34]

---

[34] See Rev. Rul. 65-34, 1965-1 CB 86; Rev. Rul. 54-567 1954-2 CB 108, IRS Pub 501 (2016), pgs. 12- 13; and *Martino v. Comm.*, 71 T.C. 456, (1970).

**Example 3-4:** Assume Jane, age 23, was married on November 30, 2016. Her husband, Jason, age 28 earned $42,000 for the year as an accountant. Jane was a full-time student during 2016, supported by her parents, and did not have any earned income. Since Jane was fully supported by her parents, she meets all the qualifying child tests: (1) relationship, (2) age, (3) residency, and (4) support test making her eligible qualifying child of her parents. However, if Jane and Jason elect to file a joint return, Jane's parents cannot claim Jane as a qualifying child.

**Planning Consideration:** The family must compare benefits of (1) Jane and Jason filing as MFJ, claiming Jane's dependency exemption on a joint return or (2) Jane and Jason filing as married, filing separately, MFS allowing Jane's parents to claim her dependency exemption if all dependency requirements are satisfied. This should be done before returns are filed, since a MFJ return cannot be amended to MFS, but MFS returns can later be amended to a MFJ return.[35]

---

[35] Reg. Sec. 1.6013 (a).

**Planning Consideration:** Assume Jason from the above example had only $10,000 of earned income during 2016, as he could not find a full-time job during 2016. Jane was a full-time student during 2016, supported by her parents. Jane and Jason can file a joint return, as the $10,000 of total income will be offset by a $12,600 standard deduction, reducing taxable income to zero. Jason and Jane must also have a zero tax liability on each married filing separately return in order to file married filing jointly. Jason's $10,000 of earned income would be offset by a $6,200 MFS standard deduction and a $4,050 personal exemption. Jane's parents can claim her as a qualifying child, as all the qualifying child tests are satisfied. Jason and Jane's joint return is filed to obtain a refund of Jason's withholding and is considered a refund claim.[36]

**Observation:** Sec. 152(b)(2) flatly disallows another taxpayer from claiming an exemption when a married dependent files a joint return with a spouse. However, Sec. 152(c)(1)(E), covering qualified children, allows an

---

[36] Rev. Rul. 54-567, 1954-2 CB 108; Rev Rul. 1965-1 CB 86, and *Martino, William,* (1978) 71 TC 456, acq. (1979) 1979-2 CB 2.

exception to this exemption disallowance by allowing a dependency exemption when a married dependent files a joint return with a spouse to claim a refund. Sec. 152(c)(1)(E) makes no mention the married dependent and his or her spouse must have no tax liability on the basis of a separate return. The IRS and Tax Court require no tax liability exist on a separate return.[37]

## Dependents of another Taxpayer/Dependents Filing MJF Return-Surviving Spouse

These two tests, previously discussed, and the gross income test for qualifying relatives (Sec. 152 (d)(1)(H)) are not applied in determining if a surviving spouse has a dependent for purposes of filing as a qualifying widow(er). Sec. 2(a) defining a surviving spouse specifically provides in Sec. 2(a)(1)(B) that the surviving spouse must maintain a home and household that is the principal place of abode as a member of such household "…of a dependent (1) who within the meaning of Sec. 152, determined without regard to subsections (b)(1), (b)(2), and (d)(1)(H) thereof…" The waiver of the application of these requirements may allow a surviving spouse to file as a qualifying widow(er) while his or her dependent could have dependents on the dependent's return and/or file MFJ with his or her spouse. For more discussion of this issue, see "Tax Issues Facing a Surviving Spouse" by

---

[37] Id.

Mark Nielsen and James M. Hopkins in the October 2017 issue of Practical Tax Strategies, Volume 99, No. 4, pages 34-39.

## Citizenship

A dependent must be a citizen or National of the United States, a resident of the United States[38], or a resident of a country contiguous (Canada or Mexico) to the United States at some time during the calendar year in which the taxpayer's tax year begins.[39] U.S citizens or U.S. Nationals who have legally adopted a child who is not a U.S. citizen, U.S. resident alien, or U.S. National satisfy this test for a child who is not a U.S. citizen (1) if the child was a member of the taxpayer's household for the entire year, (2) the child had the same principal abode as the taxpayer, and (3) the taxpayer is a U.S. citizen or U.S. National. This rule also applies to any child lawfully placed with the taxpayer for adoption.[40] It isn't necessary the child in this situation be adopted for the entire year, it is necessary the child live with the taxpayer for the entire year.[41]

---

[38] See IRC Sec. 7701 (b) for the definition of a resident alien.

[39] IRC Sec. 152 (b)(3)(A); IRS Pub 17 (2016), p 26; and Reg. Sec. 1.152-2(a).

[40] Id.

[41] Reg. Sec. 152-2(a)(2)(ii).

Children born to a U.S. citizen are a U.S. citizen even if the other parent is a nonresident alien and the children were born in a foreign country.[42]

> **Example 3-5:** Children born to a U.S. citizen living abroad with a nonresident alien spouse are considered U.S. citizens. They can be claimed as dependents if all dependency conditions, discussed later, are satisfied.[43]

> **Example 3-6:** Herman, a U.S. citizen and calendar year taxpayer is employed in Japan. In July 2013, he takes Samantha, a citizen of Japan, into his home for the purpose of legally adopting her. Samantha lives with Herman and his family for the rest of 2013 and all of 2014. The adoption is completed in 2014. If all the other dependency rules are satisfied, Samantha is a dependent on Herman's 2014 tax return. Samantha does not qualify as a dependent for 2013, as she was not a member of the Herman's household for the entire taxable year.

---

[42] Id. and Rev. Rul. 71-44, 1971-1 CB 49.

[43] IRC Sec. 152 (b)(3((A).

**Example 3-7:** In *Jan J. Wexler*, T.C. Memo 1974-113, taxpayer challenged the constitutionality of then IRC Sec. 152(b)(3) denying dependency exemptions for his non-U.S. citizen and non-U.S. National parents who lived in Israel. The Tax Court upheld this code section and denied dependency exemptions for his parents.

If the dependency exemption was for a child born in the United States, making him or her a U.S. citizen, then all the other conditions of a qualifying child or qualifying relative (discussed later) would have to be satisfied to claim a dependency exemption.

**Example 3-8:** In *Leah Carlebach, et.vir. v. Commissioner,* 139 T.C. No 1 and *Daniel Stern et.ux. v. Commissioner,* TC Memo 2012-204, decided on the same day, covered children who were not U.S. citizens at the end of the tax year. One parent in each case was a U.S. citizen but the children were born in Israel. Taxpayers argued the children were American citizens by default since one parent in each case was a U.S. citizen. In these cases, to qualify as a U.S. citizen, a child must be born in the United States or receive naturalization through treaty

36

or by Congressional authority. Lacking birth in the United States and the failure by the parents to apply for naturalization for the children to receive a certificate of naturalization before the end of the tax year for which benefits are claimed, the taxpayers could not claim exemptions for the children. Once the parents obtained the children's certificates of naturalization, the children qualified as U.S. citizens for the year the certificates were obtained and thereafter.

**Planning Consideration:** If a taxpayer lives outside the United States, tax preparers should ask if taxpayer's children were born outside the United States, and ask for the children's certificate of citizenship if the answer is affirmative.

U.S. Nationals are individuals who are not U.S. citizens, but owe his or her loyalty to the United States. American Samoans and Northern Mariana Islander residents are included in this category. [44] [45]

---

[44] See 8 U.S.C. Sec. 1101 (a)(22) and *Pike-Biegunski v. Commissioner,* T.C. Memo 1984-288 for the definition of a National.

[45] IRS Pub 17 (2016), p 27.

Foreign students participating in a qualified international education exchange program for a temporary period are not considered U.S. residents and cannot be claimed as exemptions.[46]

## Effect of Proposed Regulations on Qualifying Child and Qualifying Relative

The proposed regulations make extensive changes to existing Sec. 152 regulations to update them for WFTRA changes passed in 2004 and incorporate the WFTRA provisions. Readers are directed to read the proposed regulations for specific issues. Limited highlights will be shown here. The general rules section for dependents in the proposed regulations cover:

1. Support
   a. Regulations discuss various types of support, when unpaid or future support is counted as support, government payments, medical care payments, and scholarships.
   b. The regulations list types of support provided by third parties and that Social Security benefits and Social Security survivor and disability benefits are treated as support provided

---

[46] Id.

by the child to the extent used for the child's support.

c. Government payments including the Social Security benefits described above received for the support of another individual and used for that purpose are considered support provided by the recipient and are not considered provided by a third party.

d. Medical insurance premiums, including premiums for Medicare parts A to D are considered support while Medicare Parts A to D benefits are not considered support.

e. Scholarships provided to a student who is the child of a taxpayer are not treated as an item of support.

2. Relationship test

a. Discusses a joint return and divorce or death of spouse.

b. Taxpayer filing a joint return and claiming an individual as a QC or QR can claim such individual even if the spouse has no described relationship with the dependent individual.

c. A relationship between a taxpayer and an individual created by marriage and claimed as a dependent by the taxpayer continues after the termination of the marriage or death.

3. Principal place of abode
   a. Discusses temporary absence, residing with taxpayer for more than one-half the taxable year, including six examples regarding principal place of abode.

4. Special circumstances causing part year residence
   a. Discusses when a dependent is born or dies during the year, and issues related to an adopted or foster child, including when the child is not a citizen or national of the United States.

5. Missing child
   a. Discusses issues related to both a qualifying child and qualifying relative who law enforcement presume has been kidnapped by someone who is not a member of the family of either the child or taxpayer.

## Effect of Proposed Regulations on (QC) and (QR) Dependents applicable to Sec. 152(e)

Sec. 152(e) provides special rules to dependents when the parents are divorced, separated, or live apart. The proposed regulations discuss how a noncustodial parent can file Form 8332 or written declaration to claim a child for a dependency exemption and child tax credit.

The regulations provide that a noncustodial parent may submit a copy of the written declaration during an examination or attached to an amended return to substantiate a claim to the dependency exemption. If the custodial parent signed the written declaration after he or she filed a return claiming a dependency exemption, the custodial parent must file an amended return to remove a previously claimed dependency exemption for the child to allow the noncustodial to claim the dependency exemption. (Proposed Reg. Sec. 1-152-5(e).

Three examples illustrate the application of this provision. No amended return is required by the custodial spouse when the tax return of each parent is timely filed, including on extension. The issue of how the custodial spouse removes the previously claimed exemption is not discussed, except to state the custodial spouse is not entitled to a dependency exemption for the child. Apparently, it will be by IRS correspondence.

**Chapter 4**

**Qualifying Children**

**Background**

Congress passed The Working Families Tax Relief Act in 2004 (WFTRA) creating the qualifying child (QC) and qualifying relative (QR) designations for dependency exemptions, effective for tax years beginning after December 31, 2004. The Act created a qualifying child definition under Sec. 152(c) for determining a taxpayer's eligibility for the following child related tax benefits:

- Child and dependent care credit
- Dependent care benefits income exclusion
- Child tax credit
- Dependency exemption
- Earned income credit, and
- Head of household filing status, if applicable.

WFTRA also created a qualifying relative (QR) as a second category of dependency exemptions. This category was created to retain the dependency exemption rules in effect before the WFTRA change (tax years beginning in 2004 and prior). The QR exemption tests are in Sec. 152(d).

The following table summarizes the tests for both QC and QR dependency exemptions.

| Tests for both QC and QR Dependents | Tests for Qualifying Children (QC) | Tests for Qualifying Relatives (QR) |
|---|---|---|
| No dependents on QC's or QR's personal return 152(b)(1) | Relationship test 152(c)(2) | Dependent is not a qualifying child of any other taxpayer 152(d)(1)(D) |
| Separate return/no joint return 152(b)(2) (Married dependents only) | Age test 152(c)(3) | Relationship test 152(d)(2) |
| Citizenship/residency 152 (b)(3)(A) | Principal place of abode test 152(c)(1)(B) | Abode test for dependent unrelated to claimant 152 (d)(2)(H) |
| Identification number 151(e) | Dependent provides less than half of own support 152(c)(1)(D) | Gross income less than exemption amount 152(d)(1)(B) |
| | | Claimant provides over half of support |

References in the table are to the applicable sections of the Internal Revenue Code

The tests for both QC and QR dependency exemptions (Column 1 in the above table) were discussed previously.

Each of the tests for the QC and QR categories of dependency exemptions will be discussed in the pages that follow, starting with the QC tests.

The QC tests consist of the following:

44

- A relationship test
- An age test
- A principal place of abode, and
- A support test.

## QC Relationship Test

A qualifying child with respect to a taxpayer claiming a dependency exemption (claimant) must be individuals who:

- are children of the taxpayer: natural, step, adopted, and eligible foster[47],
- are siblings (brothers, sisters, stepbrothers, stepsisters)
- any descendants of the above[48].

> **Observation:** The QC relationship is much broader than the "child of the taxpayer" definition, discussed later. The broader test includes the claiming of taxpayer's grandchildren, great grandchildren, natural and stepsiblings, children, grandchildren, and great grandchildren of the claiming taxpayer's siblings.

---

[47] IRC Sec. 152(c)(2)(A) and 152(f)(1)(A), (B), and (C).

[48] IRC Sec. 152(c)(2)(B).

A more limited test within Sec 152 defines a child[49] of the claiming taxpayer as:

- a daughter, son, stepson or stepdaughter[50]
- an eligible foster child[51] or
- an adopted child[52].

> **Observation:** The "child of the taxpayer" is limited to taxpayer's children who are (biological or step), adopted, or eligible foster.

> **Observation:** A recent case illustrates the difference between an "eligible foster child" and adopted child exemption. In *Jean Cowan, v. Comm. of Internal Revenue*, T.C. Memo 2015-85, May 5, 2015, taxpayer, Cowan, was a guardian of Woods who lived with her when he was six weeks old, turning age 18 in 2004, and continued to live with Cowan past age 18, and was age 25 in 2011. Woods fathered a daughter in 2006. Woods and his daughter lived with Cowan during 2011 with Cowan providing most of the household support. Cowan treated Wood's daughter as her "granddaughter" as a

---

[49] IRC Sec. 152 (f)(1)(A) and (i and ii) in that subsection.

[50] IRC Sec. 152 (f)(1)(A)(i).

[51] IRC Sec. 152 (f)(1)(A)(ii) and IRC Sec. 152 (f)(1)(C).

[52] IRC Sec. 152 (f)(1)(B).

qualifying child, claiming earned income credit, child tax credit, and claimed head of household filing status. Taxpayer claimed Woods was her "eligible foster child" as defined in Sec. 152(f)(1)(c) that would treat Wood's daughter as Cowan's "granddaughter". A provision in the Ohio law stipulated a guardianship appointed for a minor before age fourteen continues until the age of majority, removal for good cause, or the ward selects another guardian. Because of the termination of the guardianship when Woods turned age 18, Cowan did not have a qualifying child for the previously mentioned child tax benefits originally claimed for her purported "granddaughter". However, she was allowed a qualifying relative exemption for Woods, as he lived with her for the entire twelve months of 2011 and satisfied all the QR tests, while the purported "granddaughter" was absent from the household for one month that was not identified as temporary. Because of the one-month absence, the granddaughter could not qualify for as a qualifying relative.

Had Cowan adopted Woods as a minor or later as an adult, then he would have been her son and qualified as a blood relative[53] and Wood's daughter would have been Cowan's granddaughter, giving her the result on her originally filed return.

**Observation:** A "child of the taxpayer" does not include grandchildren of claiming taxpayer, while the QC definition includes grandchildren, by including the phrase, "a child's descendant". A "child of the taxpayer", who is a full-time student, does not have to count college scholarships in his or her support test.[54] However, this benefit would not apply to a taxpayer's grandchild in the same situation, as this exclusion of the scholarship only applies to a "child of the taxpayer".

---

[53] Id.

[54] IRC Sec. 152(f)(5).

The following table lists the relationships satisfying the QC and QR definitions. The QR provisions are shown to easily compare both definitions.

| Qualifying children (QC) | Qualifying Relatives (QR) |
|---|---|
| Children and their descendants 152 (c)(2)(A) | Children and their descendants 152 (d)(2)(A) |
| Brothers, sisters, stepbrothers, stepsisters, or their descendants 152 (c)(2)(B) | Brothers, sisters, stepbrothers, stepsisters, or their descendants 152 (d)(2)(B) |
| Eligible foster children 152 (f)(1)(A)(ii) and 152 (f)(1)(C) | Parents and their ancestors 152 (d)(2)(C) |
| Adopted children 152 (f)(1)(B) | Stepfather or stepmother 152 (d)(2)(D) |
| Half-brothers and half-sisters 152(f)(4) | Son or daughter of a brother or sister 152 (d)(2)(E) |
|  | Brothers or sisters of the father or mother 152 (d)(2)(F) |
|  | In-laws: son, daughter, father, mother, brother, and sister 152 (d)(2)(G) |
|  | Unrelated individual, other than taxpayer's spouse, who was member of taxpayer's household for entire year 152 (d)(2)(H) |

The definitions appear in the order they are discussed in Sec. 152 of the Internal Revenue Code.

**Example 4-1:** Robert's household includes his biological son, his grandson (his son's son), his nephew, his sister, his stepsister, and his stepsister's son. With respect to Robert, all of these household members satisfy the QC relationship test.

**Example 4-2:** Robert's parents and their ancestors, stepparents, in-laws, and unrelated individuals (residing with Robert for the entire year) meet the QR relationship test.

**Observation:** Cousins do not meet the relationship test for qualifying child. A cousin can be claimed as a qualifying relative (discussed later) provided the cousin's principal place of abode is the taxpayer's home and the cousin is a member of the claimant's household for the entire taxable year.

## Age Test

The second of the four tests is the age test. A QC must satisfy one of the following conditions related to age[55]:

- Be under age 19 at the end of the taxable year.
- Be under age 24 at the end of the tax year and a full-time student at a qualifying educational institution for that year. Full-time status is determined by the rules and regulations of each qualified educational institution[56]. Full-time status is satisfied for some part (not full months) of five calendar months during the

---

[55] IRC 152(c)(3).

[56] IRS Pub 501 (2016), Exemptions, Standard Deduction, and Filing Information, p 13.

calendar year that do not have to be consecutive months[57]. Educational institutions "include primary and secondary schools, college, universities, normal schools, technical schools, mechanical schools, and similar institutions, but do not include non-educational institutions, on-the-job training, correspondence schools, night schools, and so forth."[58] Internet only courses would also not qualify even if enrolled for a full-time load.

- Any age if totally and permanently disabled[59]. In this situation, the age test does not apply.
- The QC must be younger than the claiming taxpayer.[60]

**Observation:** The under age 19 condition applies to children who are high school age or younger.

---

[57] Id.

[58] Reg. Sec. 1.151-3(c).

[59] IRC Sec. 152(c)(3)(B) effective with years starting in 2005 by the Working Families Tax Relief Act, Public Law 108-311 enacted in 2004.

[60] The requirement a QC had to be younger than the claiming taxpayer was enacted by the Fostering Connections to Success and Increasing Adoptions Act (P. L. 110-351), effective for tax years beginning after December 31, 2008. This condition did not apply for tax years 2005-2008.

**Observation:** The under age 24 and a full-time student condition provides a way for parents of college students to claim their children as dependents provided all the other QC tests are satisfied.

**Example 4-3:** A child age 18 or younger at the end of the calendar year meets this test. If over age 18, the child must be a full-time student for five months during the year.

**Example 4-4:** Josh, age 22, shared his residence for the entire year with his 28-year-old sister, Lisa, who has been unemployed for most of the 2016 tax year. Her gross income for 2016 was $3,500. Lisa does not provide more than one-half of her own support. Lisa meets the relationship, abode (discussed later), and support tests with respect to Josh; however, Josh cannot claim her as a qualifying child dependent as she fails two aspects of the age test: She is over 24, and is older than Josh, the potential claimant. When a potential dependent fails the qualifying child test, he or she should be tested as a qualifying relative.

**Observation:** If Josh was 28 and Lisa was 22 and a full time student, Josh could claim Lisa as a qualifying child, provided she is a full-time student to satisfy the age test. She is younger than the claimant, so the second age test in the above example does not apply.

**Example 4-5:** Assume Lisa's parents file a joint return for 2016. Their daughter, Lisa, age 25, had to quit her job in April 2016 because of illness. She returned home to live with her parents for the rest of 2016. She earned $9,000 prior to quitting her job and had no additional earnings for 2016. Her parents provide over one-half her support during 2016.

Lisa meets the relationship test, the abode test over six months (discussed later), and the support test by providing less than one-half her support (discussed later). Lisa satisfies the relationship test, the abode test, but does not satisfy the age requirement, and, as a result, she is not a qualifying child. As will be discussed in the qualifying relative section, her gross income for the year exceeds the personal exemptions amount of $4,050 for 2016 and 2017; she is not a qualifying relative dependent.

If Lisa was permanently and totally disabled at any time during the year that is expected to last or can be expected to last continuously for at least one year or can lead to death, the age test would not apply, and she would be a qualifying child dependent[61]. The disability must be permanent and total disability.

**Residency (Abode) Test**

A qualifying child must have the same principal place of abode (that is, place of residence) as the claiming taxpayer for more than one-half of the taxable year[62]. Temporary absences from the principal place of abode are permitted. These include vacation, business, illness, education, or military service. A qualifying child who lives with one parent and one or more grandparent in the same residence may create a situation where the residency test is satisfied by more than one person, and if all other qualifying child tests are satisfied, more than one person may be able to claim the dependency exemption. This situation will be discussed later in the tie-breaker section.

> **Example 4-6:** Michael, age 8, lives with his mother for 4 months, grandmother for 5 months and with an aunt for 3 months during the 2016 calendar year. He is not a qualifying

---

[61] IRS Pub 17 (2016), p 28.

[62] IRC Sec. 152(c)(1)(B).

child of any these individuals because he did not live with them for more than half the year. Only divorced or separated parents can pool their custodial time to meet an abode test. If the tests for a qualifying relative (discussed later) are satisfied, the mother, grandmother, or aunt may be able to claim Michael as a qualifying relative if all the qualifying relative tests are satisfied.

A child, who was born or died during the tax year, is treated as having lived with the taxpayer for the entire year if the taxpayer's home was the child's home for the entire time the child was alive during the year[63].

A child born alive who dies shortly after birth can be claimed as a dependent if state or local law treats the birth as a live birth, provided all other qualifying child tests are satisfied. No exemption is allowed for a stillborn child[64].

Missing or kidnapped children are treated as meeting the residency test if both of the following tests are satisfied:

- If law enforcement authorities presume the child is kidnapped by someone who is not a

---

[63] Id., IRS Pub 17 (2016), p 28.

[64] Id.

member of the taxpayer's family or the child's family, and

- In the year of the kidnapping, the child lived with the claiming taxpayer for over half the partial year before the date of the kidnapping.[65]

These two conditions apply for all years until the child is returned in determining[66]:

- a dependency deduction
- the child tax credit of IRC Sec. 24
- whether an individual is a surviving spouse or head of household, and
- the earned income credit

The rules for missing and kidnapped children ceases to apply as of the first taxable year of the taxpayer beginning after the calendar year in which it is determined the child is deceased, or if earlier, the calendar year in which the child would have attained age 18.[67]

> **Example 4-7:** Miranda, age 14, lived with her mother for the month of January during 2016. She moved in with her father on February 1. She was kidnapped on March 15, 2016. Assuming the missing/kidnapped

---

[65] IRC Sec. 152(f)(6).

[66] IRC Sec. 152(f)(6)(B).

[67] IRC Sec. 152(f)(6)(D).

children conditions are satisfied, her father will be able to meet the residency test for a qualifying child, because Miranda lived with her father for more than one-half of the time before the kidnapping. The father meets the abode test for 2016. The benefit of Miranda's qualifying child exemption would cease for her father in the father's taxable year beginning after the calendar year in which she is (1) is declared dead or (2) attains age 18.

## Residency (Abode) Test for Children of Divorced or Separated Parents, Parents Who Live Apart, or Parents Who Never Married

In most cases, due to the residency (abode) test, a child of divorced or separated parents is the qualifying child of the custodial parent. A "custodial parent" is a parent with whom the child resides for the greater number of nights during a calendar year.[68] A "noncustodial parent" is the parent who is not the custodial parent.

A child is considered as living with a parent for one night if the child sleeps:

- "At that parent's home, whether or not the parent is present, or

---

[68] Id., Pub 17 (2016), p 28.

- In the company of the parent, when the child does not sleep at a parent's home (for example, the parent and child are on vacation together)."[69]

If a child lived with each parent an equal number of nights during a year, the parent with the higher adjusted gross income is the custodial parent.[70] Staying overnight with a friend and not with either parent is treated as nights with the parent the child normally would stay with.

After a child is emancipated (reaches age 18 in most states or age 20 in some states), the child is treated as "residing with neither parent." [71]

A parent who works at night is allowed to count days a child lived with such parent instead of counting nights. If the days the child lived with such parent are greater than the nights, the night working parent is treated as the custodial parent.[72]

> **Example 4-8:** Gina's parents are divorced. Gina, age 14, lived with her father for 185 days and with her mother for 180 days. Her father is the custodial parent.

---

[69] Id.

[70] Id.

[71] Reg. Sec. 1.152-4(d)(1).

[72] Id., Pub 17 (2016), p 28.

**Observation:** Parents and tax preparers must be cognizant of the number of days of custody for each parent to insure which parent is treated as the custodial parent. This should be a tax planning consideration in the last month of the tax year, usually December, if the total days for each parent are about equal.

**Example 4-9:** Assume the Gina lived with each parent exactly 180 days each, and it cannot be determined with which parent she lived for the five remaining days in the calendar year. In this situation, the parent with the higher adjusted gross income is considered the custodial parent.[73]

**Example 4-10:** Assume Gina, instead of being age 14, turned age 18 on May 15 of the calendar year, and is considered emancipated in the state of her residence. She is not considered in the custody of either parent for more than half of the year. As a result, the special rule for children of divorced or separated parents does not apply. Gina's dependency exemption would

---

[73] Id., Example 3, p 28.

be subject to the residency (abode) test of IRC Sec. 152(c)(1)(B) for the applicable parent.[74]

**Example 4-11:** Assume Gina turned age 18 in September 15 of the tax year, and is considered emancipated in the state of her residence. She is not treated as in the custody of either parent on September 15. The custodial parent test is based on the number of days Gina lived with each parent for the days from January 1 to September 14. For subsequent years, Gina would be subject to all qualifying child or qualifying relative tests depending on her individual situation.

A child can be treated as a qualifying child of the noncustodial spouse if all four of the following conditions are true.

1) "The parents:[75]
   a. Are divorced or legally separated under a decree of divorce or separate maintenance,
   b. Are separated under a written separation agreement, or

---

[74] Id., Example 5, p 28.

[75] Id., Pub 17 (2016), p 28.

       c.  Lived apart at all times during the last 6 months of the year, whether or not they are or were married.

2) The child received over half of his or her support for the year from the parents.
3) The child is in the custody of one or both parents for more than half of the year.
4) Either of the following is true.

       a.  The custodial parent signs a written declaration, discussed later, that he or she will not claim the child as a dependent for the year, and the noncustodial parent attaches this written declaration to his or her return.

       b.  A pre-1985 decree of divorce or separate maintenance or written separation agreement that applies to the current tax year states the noncustodial parent can claim the child as a dependent, the decree or agreement was not changed after 1984 to say the noncustodial parent cannot claim the child as a dependent, and the noncustodial parent provides at least $600 for the child's support during the year."

**Example 4-12:** Gina's parents are divorced. Gina, age 14, lived with her father for 185 days and with her mother for 180 days. Her father is the custodial parent. Assuming that Gina's father signs Form 8332, her mother attaches such form to her tax return, and all of the requirements for allowing the noncustodial parent to take Gina as an exemption are satisfied, Gina's mother can claim Gina as an exemption, the child tax credit, and additional child tax credit.[76]

**Example 4-13:** Gina's parents are divorced. Gina, age 14, lived with her father for 185 days and with her mother for 180 days. Her father is the custodial parent. Assume Gina's father did not sign Form 8332. As a result, IRC Sec. 152(e), the special rule of allowing the noncustodial parent to claim a child's dependency exemption, does not apply, since Form 8332 was not issued. Gina's dependency exemption is determined by section 152(c) or (d), depending on whether she is

---

[76] Reg. Sec. 1-152-4(g), Example 1 and Form 8332.

respectively, a qualifying child or qualifying relative.[77]

**Observation:** If the first three, (1, 2, and 3) of the four conditions listed above related to assigning the dependency exemption to a noncustodial parent are satisfied, the child is a qualifying child or qualifying relative of one of the parents, and regardless of whether of a Form 8332 is filed, the child is considered a dependent of both parents for the following purposes:

- The child's receipt of a parent's employer-provided health care plan
- Contributions to an accident or health plan by a parent's employer on behalf of the child
- The child's use of a fringe benefit that qualifies as a no-additional-cost service or qualified employee discount,
- The child's deductible medical expense, and
- The child's qualified medical expenses paid from health savings accounts (HSA)

---

[77] Id., Example 2.

distributions or Archer medical savings account that are excludable from gross income.[78]

Reg. section 1.152-4 contains additional examples related to exemptions for children of divorced or separated parents. In addition, the special rule for divorced or separated parents also applies to parents who never married and who live apart at all times during the last 6 months of the year.[79]

If the decree or separation agreement went into effect after 2008, the noncustodial parent must obtain a custodial parent signed Form 8332 or similar statement whose only purpose is to release the custodial parent's claim to an exemption for the child. Form 8332 or similar statement must be unconditional, and not depend on paying child support. The noncustodial parent must attach such form or similar statement to his or her tax return in order to claim an exemption for the child.

If the decree or separation agreement went into effect after 1984 and before 2009, the noncustodial parent may be able to attach certain pages from the decree or separation agreement instead of attaching Form 8332. For this period of decrees and separation agreements, the decree or separation agreement must state all of the following:

---

[78] IRS Rev. Proc. 2008-48, 2008-36 I.R.B. 586.

[79] IRS Pub 17 (2016), p 29.

1) The noncustodial parent can claim the child as a dependent without regard to any condition, such as paying child support
2) The custodial parent will not claim the child as a dependent for the year, and
3) The years for which the noncustodial parent, rather the custodial parent, can claim the child as a dependent.

The noncustodial parent must attach all of the following pages of the decree or separation agreement to his or her tax return:

a. The cover page showing the hand written social security number of the other parent
b. The pages showing the information in steps 1) through 3) above, and
c. The signature page with the other parent's signature and the date of the agreement.

**Observation:** The release of dependency exemption to the noncustodial parent allows that person to claim (1) the dependency exemption, (2) the child tax credit, (3) the additional child tax credit, and (4) any education credits attributable to education expenses paid for the child by the noncustodial parent.[80]

A custodial spouse can revoke a written declaration that allows the noncustodial parent to the dependency exemption and other benefits mentioned above. The written notice to revoke must be given to the noncustodial parent. The effective date of the revocation begins the first calendar year after the written notice is provided. The revocation can be made on Form 8332 or a successor form designed by the IRS. The specific year or years of the revocation must be shown.

> **Example 4-14:** A custodial parent who provides a revocation of the written declaration in the 2016 tax year will be effective on January 1, 2017, the first calendar year after the written notice is provided to the noncustodial parent.

---

[80] The release of the dependency exemption to the noncustodial spouse allows these benefits to the noncustodial parent, since they all require that an exemption be claimed on a tax return. Tuition deductions and education credits follow the dependency exemption. See Form 8332 and Pub 970, p 18, under the section, Who Can Claim a Dependent's Expenses?

## Support Test

A qualifying child cannot provide over one-half his or her own support for the tax year.[81] This test is different than the support test of qualifying relative that will be discussed later.

In determining support provided by the claiming taxpayer and the qualifying child, the claiming taxpayer must compare the support he or she provided to the amount of support provided by all sources. The key test is the qualifying child cannot contribute over one-half of his/her own support and satisfy the support test.

Some, but not a complete list of support items, consists of clothing, education, food, lodging, medical and dental care, recreation, transportation, and other necessities. Support items are valued at the amount expended, except lodging is valued at fair value of lodging.

Foster care payments provided by a child placement agency, state or county are considered provided by that source.[82] Social Security survivor benefits paid to a child for the loss of a parent are not counted for support if the benefits are not spent for the child's support.[83]

---

[81] IRC Sec. 152(c)(1)(D).

[82] IRS Pub 17 (2016), pgs. 29 and 34.

[83] Id., p. 34 and Rev. Rul. 57-344, 1957-2 CB 112. (Rev. Rul. 57-344 will be obsolete by the proposed regulations.)

Scholarships provided to a full-time student for tuition, books, fees, supplies, and equipment are not taken into account in determining whether a child provided more than one-half of his or her own support. Such amounts are excluded from the support provided the student and support provided by his or her parents. This exclusion applies to a child of the taxpayer only.[84] If the claiming taxpayer was not a child's parent, but a grandparent or sibling, the qualifying child must count any scholarships as support they provide.

A child's scholarship for other than tuition, books, fees, supplies, and equipment, such as for room and board, would be considered income to the child and support provided by the child.[85] Amounts received as G.I Bill benefits are not considered scholarships and are included in the support test as support provided by the recipient.[86]

Loans taken out by a qualifying child where he or she is personally responsible for the loan are counted as support provided by the qualifying child.[87]

---

[84] IRC Sec. 152(f)(5).

[85] IRC Sec. 117 (b)(2).

[86] Reg. Sec. 1.152-1(c).

[87] IRS Pub 17 (2016), p 30, Worksheet 3-1 and *McCauley, Philip J.,* (1971) 56 TC 48, and IRS Pub 501 (2016), pg. 20.

Funds earned by a qualifying child are counted in the support determination only if the child expends them for his or her support. Income earned by the child that is saved and not expended for support is not counted in the support calculation.

Wages paid to a qualifying child by a claiming taxpayer and expended by the child for his or her support are considered provided by the child and are not considered contributed by the claiming taxpayer.[88] Support items are included in the year the money is expended for the support item, and not when paid in a later year if borrowed in the previous year.

## Special Rules for One Qualifying Child of More Than One Person

When a child lives with both parents for more than six months of the year, who file married filing jointly, the child is a qualifying child of his or her parents and no one else.[89] In some situations, a child may live with one or more parent, a grandparent, and possibly an aunt or uncle in the same household for the entire year. In such situation the child may meet the relationship, age, (abode) residency, support, and joint return tests and be a qualifying child of more than one person in that same household. While the child could be a qualifying child of each of these persons, only one person can treat the child as a qualifying child and take the following tax benefits for the child:

---

[88] Id., p 34.

[89] IRS Pub 17 (2016), p 31.

- Child and dependent care credit,
- Dependent care benefits income exclusion,
- Child tax credit,
- Dependency exemption,
- Earned income credit, and
- Head of household filing status, if applicable.

The person eligible to claim the child as a qualifying child is entitled to all of the above benefits, with no benefits to any other person. The assignment of the benefits to one person prevents sharing among more than one person to shift such benefits between eligible persons. The other person may qualify for benefits if another qualifying child lived in the same household and satisfied the previously mentioned qualifying child tests.

It is critical to plan what benefits are available to each eligible claimant when more than one claimant can claim a dependency exemption if a parent cannot claim the exemption or if the parents of the dependent have the choice of selecting which parent can claim the dependent. In the case of benefits to the parent, this would be if they are not married, filing as single. If married and they do not file married filing jointly, then they must file as married filing separately and would have to determine which party reaps the most benefits.[90] Married filing jointly would require

---

[90] Married filing separately means head of household may not be available, no earned income credit, and no credit for

calculating benefits for both parents and for any other eligible person who has a higher AGI that is more than one-half the AGI on the MFJ return of the parents.[91]

In order to have a means of determining which person can treat the child as a qualifying child and claim the six tax benefits, a set of rules, called tie-breaker rules, apply in such situation. The tie-breaker rules are summarized as follows:[92]

| More than one person is eligible to claim the same qualifying child, and the following condition applies: | The child is treated as the qualifying child of the following person |
|---|---|
| 1. Only one of the eligible persons is the child's parent | The parent is entitled to claim the child |
| 2. Parents file a separate return, each claiming the child as a qualifying child | The IRS will allow the parent with whom the child lived with for the longer period of time during the year |
| 3. Parents file a separate return, each claiming the child as a qualifying child. Child lives with each parent an equal amount of time during the year | Parent with higher AGI is allowed to claim the child |
| 4. None of the eligible persons are the child's parents | Eligible person with the higher AGI |

---

child and dependent care expenses. IRS Pub 17 (2016), p 31, Example 7.

[91] Id., Example 6.

[92] Id., p 31, and IRC Sec. 152(c)(4). The tie-breaker rules were amended by P.L. 110-351, Fostering Connections to Success and Increasing Adoptions Act, effective for tax years beginning after 2008.

The parent(s) and other persons entitled to claim a child as a qualifying child may be able to choose which person can claim the child as a qualifying child. If they cannot agree and two or more claim benefits for the same child, the tie-breaker rules become mandatory.

The tie-breaker rules will be illustrated using several examples, applying the amendments made to the tie-breaker rules made by P.L. 110-351.

**Common Facts:**

> **Example 4-15:** For 2016, assume Carly, or C, is a 10-year-old child who lives the entire year with her unmarried mother, M, and her grandmother, G. C meets the age, relationship, support (provides less than one-half), and abode tests for M (mother) and for G (grandmother), making her a qualifying child for each party and nobody else. Further, assume that M and G's AGI is $15,000 and $20,000 respectively. Assume that C is not a qualifying child of her father, as he did not live in the household for over one-half the year. Assume the rule for divorced or separated parents who live apart that allows the custodial parent the ability to assign Carly's dependency exemption to the noncustodial parent does not apply because C's father did not provide over one-half of C's support.

The mother has two choices in this situation. M can claim Carly as her qualifying child and all related tax benefits, or, since G's AGI is higher at $20,000, can allow G to claim Carly and all related tax benefits.[93] All of the previously mentioned tax benefits are allowed to the person claiming the dependency exemption for the child. The other eligible person cannot take any of these benefits. This is an application of the fourth option on the priority of tie breaker rules.

**Example 4-16:** Assume M's AGI is $25,000 instead of the previously mentioned $15,000. M must claim Carly as her dependent and all the related tax benefits. She cannot allow G these benefits because G's AGI is lower at $20,000 than M's AGI.[94] This is an application of the first option on the priority of the tie breaker rules. Rules 2, 3 and 4 do not apply in this situation.

**Example 4-17:** If M and G cannot agree on who can take C as a qualifying child, and they both claim her, the tie-breaker rules are mandatory. The first

---

[93] IRS Pub 17 (2016), p 31, Example 1.

[94] Id., Example 2.

tie-breaker rule applies giving C's exemption and all related tax benefits to M, her mother, as a parent.[95]

**Example 4-18:** Assume M has AGI is $15,000 and G has $20,000 for AGI, the facts of the first example. M has the ability to forgo claiming Carly as a dependent, since her AGI is less than G's. Assume that M's aunt, A, has also lived in the same household for the entire year. A's AGI is $25,000 for the year. The aunt is also a person eligible to claim all of Carly's tax benefits. If M elects to forgo Carly's tax benefits and allow another person to claim those benefits, it would have to be the aunt, since the aunt's AGI is higher than G's AGI.

**Example 4-19:** Assume that B, age 7, a second child of M, also lives in the household for the entire year with G and M. B is not a qualifying child of his father. B meets all the tests to be a qualifying child of M and G for the year. In this case, M would have to claim both children if her AGI is greater than G's AGI. If G's AGI is higher, M can allow G to take one or both

---

[95] Id., Example 3.

children. If G claims both children, M would not have any benefits available. If M and G each claim one child, each would receive benefits of one child.[96]

**Example 4-20:** Assume M is 18 or under or a full-time student under age 24, lives with her child, C, and lives with G in G's household for the entire year. M and C do not provide over half their own support. Assuming other QC requirements are satisfied, M and C are QC of G. As a result, M cannot claim C as a dependent because taxpayers claimed on another taxpayer's return cannot claim any dependents.[97]

**Example 4-21:** Assume that M and her husband, H, live with C and G in the same household for the entire year.   C meets the age, relationship, support test, and abode tests for her parents and for G. If M and H do not claim C as a dependent on a MFJ return, G may claim C for all of the tax benefits if G's AGI is higher than the one-half the combined AGI on M and H's MFJ return.[98]

---

[96] Id., Example 4.

[97] Id., Example 5.

[98] Id., Example 6. The AGI on the MFJ return is divided into two equal parts, and then compared to the AGI of the

**Example 4-22:** Assume that M and H, lived together as a married couple until August 1, 2016. G did not live in the household. H moved out and lived separately. C lived with M for August and September, then with H, her father, from October to December 31, 2016. C meets the age, abode, relationship, and support tests, for both M and H. At the end of the year, M and H were not divorced, legally separated, or separated under a written separation agreement, so the rule for children of divorced or separated parents or parents who live apart does not apply. M and H will file as MFS. If H allows M to take C as a qualifying child, M will receive a dependency exemption, child tax credit, and exclusion of dependent care benefits, if otherwise qualified. Head of household is not available to H or M, as they did not live apart for the last 6 months of the year. Earned income credit and child and dependent care expenses (credit) are not available when MFS.[99] The higher AGI tie-breaker rule

_____

other eligible person to determine which eligible person has the higher AGI.

[99] Id., p 31, Example 7.

does not apply to each party, since each party involved is a parent.

**Example 4-23:** Assume the facts in the above example (4-22), except H and M cannot agree who should get the benefits of claiming C as a qualifying child and both claim her on MFS returns. The tie-breaker rules are mandatory in such situation. The second of the tie-breaker rules applies; giving C's qualifying child benefits to H, as she lived with him for more days during the year than with M. H is entitled to a dependency exemption, child tax credit, and the exclusion of dependent care benefits. No head of household is available, since H and M were not separated in the last 6 months of the year. Earned income credit and child and dependent care benefits are not available when MFS.[100]

**Example 4-24:** If H and M in Example 4-23, above, are not married, lived together for all of 2016 with their biological child, C, age 10. C meets relationship, residency (abode), support, and age tests to be both H and M's qualifying child. Assume H's AGI

---

[100] Id., p 31, Example 8.

is \$16,000 and M's AGI is lower at \$12,000. H can elect to allow M to claim all of C's qualifying child benefits. H forgoes all of C's qualifying child benefits when making this choice.[101] Note a parent can forgo claiming a biological child as an exemption and related benefits even if such parent's AGI is higher than the AGI of the other spouse. The higher AGI rule does not apply to parents, unless parents cannot agree who should claim exemption and each parent claims her. (See next example) When such election is made, each party must analyze all six of the qualifying child tax benefits to see which party has the greatest benefit. As H and M are not married, each will file as single, so the earned income credit and child and dependent care are not disallowed as they would be for MFS.

**Example 4-25** Same facts as Example 4-24, except H and M, filing as single, since they are unmarried, each claim C's tax benefits. The third tie-breaking rule will apply and allow the person, H, with the higher AGI all of C's tax benefits. The second tie-breaker rule

---

[101] Id., p 31, Example 9.

does not apply because C lived with each parent and equal number of days during the year.[102]     Any benefits claimed by M on her separate return will be denied.

## Application of the Tie-Breaker Rules to Divorced or Separate Parents or Parents Who Live Apart

The special rule for divorced, separated or parents who live apart allows the custodial parent to release his or her claim to a qualifying child's dependency exemption and the child tax credit. "The custodial parent, if eligible, or another eligible person retains the ability to claim the qualifying child for head of household filing status, credit for child and dependent care, the exclusion for dependent care benefits, and the earned income credit."[103]

> **Example 4-26** Sally lives with her 4-year-old son, Jack, and her mother, Cheryl, for the entire 2016 year. Assume Sally has AGI of $10,000, while Cheryl's AGI is $24,000. Sally and Jack's father were divorced prior to the 2016 calendar year. Sally has signed Form 8332 releasing Jack's dependency exemption and child tax credit to Jack's father.   Jack is a

---

[102] Id., p 32, Example 10.

[103] Id., p 32.

qualifying child for his father because Sally provided Jack's father with a completed Form 8332. Jack's father is allowed to claim Jack as a dependency exemption and for the child tax credit. Jack is a qualifying child of his mother and his grandmother for the remaining child tax benefits, head of household status, if applicable, child and dependent care credit, income exclusion for dependent care benefits, and earned income credit. Sally and her mother, Cheryl, can decide on who can take Jack as a qualifying child. Sally can allow Cheryl to claim Jack's four remaining tax benefits, since Cheryl's AGI is higher than Sally's AGI. If Sally had a $30,000 AGI and Cheryl had $24,000 for AGI, the tie-breaker rules would limit Jack's remaining tax benefits to Sally.

If Sally and Cheryl each claim Jack's remaining tax benefits, the tie-breaker rules will deny Cheryl's claim to them, as the first category of the tie-breaker rules gives them to the parent, Sally.[104]

_____

[104] Id., p 32, Examples 1, 2, and 3.

## Special Rules for a Qualifying Child of More Than One Person-Prior to Amendment by P.L 110-351

Prior to amendment by P.L. 110-351, the tie-breaker rules applied only if an individual could be and was claimed as a qualifying child by two or more taxpayers for a tax year beginning in the same calendar year. If only one eligible taxpayer claimed a child when the child was a qualifying child of more than one eligible person, the tie-breaker rules did not apply. (Conf. Rept. 108-696, P.L. 108-311, p 62)

The change contained in P.L. 110-351 applies the tie-breaking rules whenever two or more taxpayers can claim an individual as a qualifying child, whether or not both actually claim the individual.

> **Example 4-27:** For 2008, taxpayers had AGI of over $400,000 on joint return. Their two children, Justin age 15, with no income, and a 20-year-old daughter, Laura, with AGI of $20,000, who is not a full-time student, resided with their parents for the entire calendar year. The son meets the relationship, support, residency, and age tests to be a qualifying child of his parents and his 20-year-old sister. During 2008 and some years prior to 2008, his parents may not have not received any benefit of his dependency exemption (phased-out for high AGI), the child tax and earned income credits because of too

high AGI. Prior to 2009, and in 2008, the tie-breaker rules would apply to this situation, but only applied if both Laura and her parents each claimed Justin as a qualifying child. This allowed Laura to claim her brother as a qualifying child and realize the benefits of Justin's qualifying child tax benefits that were lost by her parents.

The P.L 100-351 change to the tie-breaker rules prevents Laura and her parents from shifting the phased-out benefits of Justin's qualifying benefits away from her parents to another eligible person by allowing it only if another eligible person has AGI greater than the parents, which is not true in the above example.

## Effect of Proposed Regulations

The proposed regulations make extensive changes to existing Sec. 152 regulations to update them for WFTRA changes passed in 2004 and incorporate the WFTRA provisions. Readers are directed to read the proposed regulations for specific issues. Limited highlights will be shown here. The general rules section for dependents in the proposed regulations:

1. Define a QC dependent
2. Discuss ineligible dependents
   a. Dependent claimed by another taxpayer cannot have any dependents.
   b. Married dependents, except to claim withheld or estimated taxes paid by dependent.
3. Discuss citizens and nationals of other countries
4. Define a child, adopted child and a foster child
5. Define an authorized placement agency
6. Define a student
7. Define a brother and sister
   a. Includes brother or sister by half blood
8. Define a parent
   a. A stepparent who has not adopted a child is not a considered a parent

The qualifying child (QC) section in the proposed regulations discuss:

1. The QC relationship test
2. Residency test
3. Age test
4. Support test
5. Joint return test
6. Qualifying Child eligible to be claimed by more than one taxpayer
7. Coordination with other provisions

a. Except to the extent that Sec. 152(e) and Sec. 1.152-5 apply, if more than one taxpayer may claim a child as a qualifying child, the child is a qualifying child of only one taxpayer for purposes of:
  i. Head of household status
  ii. The child and dependent care credit under Sec. 21
  iii. The child tax credit under Sec. 24
  iv. The earned income credit under Sec. 32
  v. The exclusion from income for dependent care assistance under Sec. 129
  vi. The dependency exemption under Sec. 151.
b. If Sec. 152(e) applies, the noncustodial parent may claim the child as a qualifying child for purposes of the dependency exemption and child tax credit, and the custodial parent may claim the child for purposes of one or more of the above provisions.

c.  Six      examples      discuss application  of  the  tiebreaker rules.

# Chapter 5

## Qualifying Relative

When Congress passed The Working Families Tax Relief Act in 2004 (WFTRA), creating the qualifying child concept for dependency exemptions, it also created a qualifying relative concept. Both of these were effective for tax years beginning after December 31, 2004.

The qualifying relative concept was a second category of dependency exemptions created to retain dependency exemptions in effect before WFTRA (tax years beginning in 2004 and prior).

The two terms are not the same[105]. Each term and its respective tests should be considered in determining a dependency exemption, starting with the tests for a qualifying child, and if that fails, tests for a qualifying relative.

---

[105] ILM 200812024, Feb 8, 2008.

The tests are:

- Dependent is not a qualifying child of any other taxpayer,
- Residency/Citizenship
- Relationship/Member of Household
- Gross income, and
- Claimant provides over one-half dependent's support.

Each test will be discussed in this chapter.

**Dependent is not a Qualifying Child of any other Taxpayer**

A child cannot be a qualifying relative if the child is the taxpayer's qualifying child or the child is a qualifying child of any other taxpayer.

> **Example 5-1:** Gina is taxpayer's 20-year-old-daughter. She is a full-time student, lives with the taxpayer, and meets all the tests to be a qualifying child of the taxpayer. She is not the taxpayer's qualifying relative.

> **Example 5-2:** If Gina was 13, lived with taxpayer for the entire year and meets all the tests for the taxpayer's qualifying child, she is not a qualifying relative.

**Example 5-3:** Gina is a taxpayer's 20-year-old daughter, who is not permanently and totally disabled. She is not a full-time student. She lived with the taxpayer for the entire year. She is not taxpayer's qualifying child, as she fails to meet the age test. She could be the taxpayer's qualifying relative if she meets the gross income and support tests.

**Example 5-4:** Taxpayer's granddaughter, age 7, lived with the taxpayer for 4 months, her mother for 3 months, and an aunt for 5 months. The granddaughter is not taxpayer's qualifying child, as she did not meet the abode test by living with the taxpayer for more than six months during the year. The granddaughter may be a qualifying relative if the gross income test and support tests are satisfied.

**Observation:** In the case of the granddaughter, above, she does not have to meet the residency test for a qualifying relative as she is related to taxpayer.

What would normally be a taxpayer's qualifying child may not be a qualifying child of any other taxpayer and may be a qualifying relative of another taxpayer provided the child's parents are not required to file a tax return and (1) do not file a return or (2) file a return only to get a refund of income tax withheld. [106]

**Example 5-5:** Taxpayer and special female friend live together for the entire year in the taxpayer's home with her 5-year-old child. Taxpayer supports female friend. Special friend has no income. She is not required to file a tax return for the year and does not file a return. The taxpayer can claim his special friend and her child as qualifying relative dependency exemptions provided all other requirements of sections 151 and 152 are satisfied. [107]

**Observation:** In this case the 5-year-old child, who normally would be the

---

[106] Notice 2008-5, 2008-2 I.R.B. 256. (Notice 2008-5 will be obsolete by the proposed regulations.) Proposed regulations, (REG-137604-07) make Notice 2008-5 obsolete. The contents on that Notice are reflected in the proposed regulations in Sec 152-3(c)(2) using three very similar examples. The IRS position in this Notice was upheld in *Danita J. Leonard, v. Commissioner,* T.C. Summary Op. 2008-141.

[107] Id., Example 1. Also refer to the proposed regulations discussed in the above footnote.

special friend's qualifying child, qualifies as the taxpayer's qualifying relative, since the mother did not have to file a tax return and did not file a return.

**Example 5-6:** Assume the special friend had $2,000 for total wages and filed a return to get a refund of income tax withheld from her wages. She does not claim earned income credit or any other tax deductions or credits. The special friend and her child are the taxpayer's qualifying relatives if the member-of-the-household, gross income and support tests are satisfied.[108] This return was filed only to claim a refund of income tax withheld from wages, and as a result, treats the child as not being a qualifying child of any other taxpayer, allowing the claiming taxpayer to treat the child as a qualifying relative.

**Example 5-7:** Assume the special friend had $2,000 of gross receipts from selling garden produce that resulted in $850 of net earnings. If the $850 is deemed self-employment income, then she is required to file a return when net

---

[108] Id., Example 2. Also refer to the proposed regulations discussed in the above footnote.

earnings from self-employment are at least $400.[109]  Because she is required to file a return, her child is her qualifying child and is no longer the supporting taxpayer's qualifying relative. Even though she is required to file a return because of net earnings from self-employment, she would still meet the gross income test, the relationship/residence test, is not a qualifying child of another taxpayer, and the support test.  With a qualifying child, she is eligible for all child tax law benefits.

While the special friend meets all the tests to be a qualifying relative mentioned above, she cannot be claimed as a qualifying relative by the supporting taxpayer because a dependent, whether a QC or QR, is treated as having no dependents.[110]

If the garden produce sales are hobby income, shown as other income on her return, she would not have to file a return.  In this case the special friend and her child would be qualifying relatives of the supporting taxpayer.

---

[109] IRC Sec. 1402(b).

[110] Sec. 152(b)(1).

**Observation:** When a child qualifies as the taxpayer's qualifying relative for a dependency exemption, he/she does not qualify the taxpayer for (1) earned income credit, (2) child tax credit, (3) child care credit (unless the qualifying relative is physical or mentally disabled)[111], and (4) exclusion of child care benefits from gross income, and (5) head-of-household filing status, if applicable. [112]

**Example 5-8:** Assume the special friend when filing a return to refund the income tax withheld had higher income and qualified for the earned income credit, which was claimed when she filed her return.  In this revised situation, her child is her qualifying child, making the child a qualifying child of the mother.  In this case, the supporting taxpayer who previously

---

[111] IRS CCA 200812024 and Sec. 21 (b)(1)(B) allow a child care credit for a qualifying relative who is physically and mentally incapable of caring for himself or herself who has the same place of abode as the claiming taxpayer for more than half of the year.

[112] ILM 200812024, Feb 8, 2008.

claimed the child as a qualifying relative cannot do so in this situation.[113]

## Residency/Citizenship Issue

A potential dependent who lives in Canada or Mexico for the entire year may not qualify as a taxpayer's qualifying child if the taxpayer lives and works in the United States, as the child does not meet the residency test (dependent must live with the taxpayer for more than one-half the year) to be a qualifying child. A potential dependent is not a qualifying child of any other taxpayer if he or she lives in Canada or Mexico with a person who is not a U.S. citizen and who has no U.S. gross income. In this case, the potential dependent may be a taxpayer's qualifying relative if the gross-income, relationship and support tests are satisfied.

> **Example 5-9:** Herman is single. He lives and works in the United States. His children, ages four and eight, live in Canada with their mother. Their mother is not a U.S. citizen and she has no U.S. source income, so she is not a U.S. taxpayer. Herman's two children are not qualifying children for dependency purposes as they fail the residency test. The children are not qualifying children

---

[113] Id., Notice 2008-5, Example 3. Also refer to the proposed regulations discussed in footnote 106.

of any other taxpayer, his mother, as she is not a U.S. taxpayer. The children are Herman's qualifying relatives if they can satisfy the gross income, relationship and support tests.[114]

Dependents who reside in a foreign country other than Canada or Mexico cannot be claimed as such unless they are a U.S. citizen, U.S. resident, or a U.S. national for some part of the year.[115] A special rule applies to an adopted child if the child, for the taxable year, has the same principal place of abode as the taxpayer and is a member of the taxpayer's household for the entire year, and the taxpayer is a citizen or national of the United States.[116]

## Relationship/Member-of-Household Test

The qualifying relative relationship/member-of-household test is broader than the relationship test for qualifying children. This broader test includes the

---

[114] Based on example in IRS Pub 17 (2016), p 27, under the Citizen or Resident Test heading.

[115] See PMTA (Program Manager Technical Assistance) 01672. It states that (1) the child tax credit is not available to a child who is not a citizen, national, or resident of the United States, (2) a dependency exemption is not allowed for a child who is not a citizen, national, or resident of the United States, nor a resident of Mexico or Canada. In addition, if the child meets all requirements for the child tax credit, the fact that the parent resides outside the United States is immaterial.

[116] IRS Sec. 152(b)(3)(A).

following individuals who are not included in the qualifying child relationship test:

- An unrelated individual who resides for the entire year as a member of the taxpayer claimant's household.
  - An unrelated individual is treated as residing in the claimant's household for temporary absences for illness, education, military service, vacation, business, and to receive constant medical care for an indefinite period in a care facility[117].
  - An unrelated individual who resides with the claimant taxpayer for the entire year does not meet the relationship test, if at any time during the year the relationship between the two parties violates local law.[118]
- The following individuals must be related to the claimant taxpayer and do not have to live with the claimant taxpayer:
  - Children, stepchildren, foster children, and their descendants-the same as for qualifying children.
    - A foster child is an individual who is placed with the taxpayer by an authorized placement

---

[117] Rev. Rul. 66-28, 1966-1 C.B. 31.

[118] IRC Sec. 152(f)(3). See IRC Sec. 152(b)(5) for tax years prior to 2005 and prior to WFTRA.

agency or by judgment, decree, or other order of any court of competent jurisdiction.[119]

- Adopted children are always treated as a taxpayer's own children. An adopted child includes one who is lawfully placed with the taxpayer for legal adoption.[120]

o Brothers, sisters, including both stepsiblings and half siblings-the same as for qualifying children.

o Parents and their ancestors, but not foster parents-not included in the qualifying children definition.

o Stepfather or stepmother-not included in the qualifying children definition

o Nephews and nieces-not included in the qualifying children definition.

o Aunts and uncles- not included in the qualifying children definition.

o In-laws, including son, daughter, father, mother, brother, and sister- not included in the qualifying children definition.

**Observation:** A cousin is not included in the qualifying relative relationship test. The only way a cousin qualifies for the relationship/member-of-

---

[119] IRC Sec. 152(f)(1)(C).

[120] IRC Sec. 152(f)(1)(B) and (C).

household test is the cousin must live in the claimant's household for the entire year.

## Other Relationship Aspects to Consider

The regulations related to Sec. 152, specifically, Reg. Sec. 1.152-2(d), states prescribed relationships can exist between either spouse on a joint return; moreover, the spouse providing support does not have to have a prescribed relationship with the person claimed as a dependent. The regulation further states, "the relationship of affinity once existing will not terminate by divorce or the death of a spouse." Please keep in mind the quoted regulation limits its application to a joint return. The following example illustrates the point that a death does not terminate the relationship.

> **Example 5-10:** Jack and Jane started supporting her widowed mother in 2008. They file joint returns. Jane passed away in 2010. Jack's mother-in-law, a U.S citizen, age 68, meets the QR relationship test, and in doing so, does not have to live with Jack to meet this test. Moreover, she is not a qualifying child of any other taxpayer. Jack may claim her as a dependent if the gross income and support tests are satisfied. The relationship of Jane's mother being Jack's mother-in-law was established before Jane's passing; it does not end when Jane passes away.

*Black's Law Dictionary*, defines affinity as, "The relationship that one spouse has to the blood relatives of the other spouse; relationship by marriage".[121] From the same source, "...There is no affinity between the blood relatives of one spouse and the blood relatives of the other. A husband is related by affinity to his wife's brother, but not to the wife of his wife's brother. There is no affinity between the husband's brother and the wife's sister..."

Rev. Rul. 71-72, 1971-1, CB 49, addressed the issue whether a taxpayer who supported the widow of his deceased wife's brother was entitled to claim her as a dependent if the taxpayer furnished her entire support. She was not a member of the taxpayer's household during the entire taxable year. The ruling denied an exemption for the sister-in-law, even though a sister-in-law was included in the relationship definition in Sec. 152 (a)(8) of the Internal Revenue Code of 1954 in effect when the ruling was issued. The ruling held the term sister-in-law was defined neither in the Code nor by regulation, the rules of affinity were controlling. In this fact situation, "a relationship of sister-in-law, a relationship of affinity, never existed between the claiming taxpayer and the widow of his deceased wife's brother."

In *Barbetti*, taxpayer filed a separate return claiming exemptions for his stepdaughter-in-law and his step grandson. The Tax Court denied the two exemptions,

---

[121] *Black's Law Dictionary, 9ᵗʰ ed.*, Bryan A. Garner, Editor-in-Chief, West Publishing, 2009, p 67.

Qualifying Relative                Other Relationship Aspects to Consider

as they were not listed in the categories of dependent relationships listed in the statute. The Court mentioned had he filed a joint return, the exemptions would have been allowed because the prescribed relationship, "In the case of a joint return it is not necessary that the prescribed relationship exist between the person claimed as a dependent and the spouse who furnishes support; it is sufficient if the prescribed relationship exists with respect to either spouse"[122]

The following individuals must meet the household test to be considered for a dependency exemption, as they do not meet the qualifying relative relationship condition:

| Individual | Support |
|---|---|
| Cousin | *Feldman v. Comm.*, 26 T.C.M. 444 (1967) |
| Aunt or uncle of a spouse | *Bates v. Comm.*, 15 T.C.M. 47 (1956) |
| Spouse of an uncle or aunt | *Koester v. Comm.*, 23 T.C. 515 (1954) |
| Spouse of a stepchild | *Barbetti v. Comm.*, 9 T.C. 1097 (1947) |
| Spouse's nephew or niece | *Grossman v. Comm.*, 26 T.C. 234 (1956) |
| Nephew or Niece's child | *Bye*, 31 T.C.M. 238, (1972) |
| Grandniece or grandnephew | *Tilney, Mary v. Comm.*, (1950) CA-5, 39 AFTR 611 |
| Non relative | *Aruai v. Comm.*, 91 T.C.M 1165 (2006) |

If a person is the claimant taxpayer's spouse at any time during the year, he or she cannot be the taxpayer's qualifying relative.[123] An individual who resides in the

---

[122] *Desio Barbetti v. Commissioner of Internal Revenue,* 9 T.C. 1097.

[123] IRC Sec. 152(d)(2)(H).

100

household to provide services is not considered a member of the taxpayer's household.[124]

> **Example 5-11:** Linda provides over one-half the support of her husband's brother, William. William is the husband's brother and Linda's brother-in-law.
> William does not have to live with Linda and her husband to meet the relationship test. If William meets all QR dependency tests, Linda and her husband can claim William as a qualifying relative if they file a joint return. Moreover, if Linda and her husband file separate returns, only Linda can claim William, as she provided over half his support.

> **Example 5-12:** A single taxpayer provides the entire support for the widow of his deceased wife's brother. She is not a member of the household for the entire year. She meets the gross income test and is not a qualifying child of any other taxpayer. The deceased wife's brother is the taxpayer's brother-in-law and would satisfy the relationship test if these facts applied to the brother-in-law. However, the issue

---

[124] *Newson v. Commissioner,* 33 T.C.M. 1188-1189 (1974).

relates to the brother-in-law's widow. The widow is not a sister-in-law of the claimant taxpayer and therefore is not a qualifying relative. A sister-in-law of the taxpayer would be a person married to the claimant taxpayer's brother, which is not the case presented here. See *Barbetti* and Rev. Rul. 71-72 previously discussed.

**Example 5-13:** Husband and wife can claim a QR dependency exemption on a joint return for the daughter of the wife's brother (the wife's niece) even if the husband furnishes a majority of the niece's support. The niece's exemption could not be claimed on the husband's separately filed return.[125]

**Observation:** A sister or brother of taxpayer's mother or father is the taxpayer's aunt or uncle. A person married to the father's sister would be the father's brother-in-law. The father's brother-in-law would not however be the taxpayer's uncle for the qualifying relative definition. The father's brother-in-law would be the

---

[125] *McCann, Russell*, (1949) 12 TC 239 and Reg. Sec. 1.152-2 (d).

taxpayer's "uncle-in-law", which is a definition not covered in IRC Sec. 152.

The following table, shown in a prior chapter, is shown again for readers to compare the differences between a qualifying child and qualifying relatives.

| Qualifying children (QC) | Qualifying Relatives (QR) |
|---|---|
| Children and their descendants 152 (c)(2)(A) | Children and their descendants 152 (d)(2)(A) |
| Brothers, sisters, stepbrothers, stepsisters, or their descendants 152 (c)(2)(B) | Brothers, sisters, stepbrothers, stepsisters, or their descendants 152 (d)(2)(B) |
| Eligible foster children 152 (f)(1)(A)(ii) and 152 (f)(1)(C) | Parents and their ancestors 152 (d)(2)(C) |
| Adopted children 152 (f)(1)(B) | Stepfather or stepmother 152 (d)(2)(D) |
| Half brothers and sisters 152(f)(4) | Son or daughter of a brother or sister 152 (d)(2)(E) |
|  | Brothers or sisters of the father or mother 152 (d)(2)(F) |
|  | In-laws: son, daughter, father, mother, brother, and sister 152 (d)(2)(G) |
|  | Unrelated individual, other than taxpayer's spouse, who was member of taxpayer's household for entire year 152 (d)(2)(H) |

The definitions appear in the order they are discussed in Sec. 152 of the Internal Revenue Code.

A stepbrother or stepsister is a child of someone who has married one of the parents. A stepbrother or stepsister is not biologically related.

A half-brother or half-sister is a child biologically related to one, but not both parents.

# Comparison of Dependency Requirements

| Test | Qualifying Child (QC) | Qualifying Relative (QR) |
|---|---|---|
| Age | Dependent must be under age 19 or a full-time student under age 24 and must be younger than claiming taxpayer. Age test does not apply to totally and permanently disabled dependents. | Does not apply |
| Gross income | Does not apply | Gross income must be less than exemption amount ($4,000 for 2015; $4,050 for 2016 and 2017). |
| Relationship | Taxpayer's child, including foster and step, siblings, half-brothers and sisters, step brothers and sisters, or any descendants of such relatives. | Taxpayer's ancestors and descendants, step parents, step siblings, nieces, nephews, aunts, uncles, in-laws, and any unrelated individual who lives with the taxpayer for the entire year. |
| Residence (Abode) | Dependent must live with taxpayer for over half the year. Temporary absences are counted as living with the claiming taxpayer | An unrelated individual must live with claiming taxpayer for the entire year. This test does not apply to others in the relationship test |
| Support | Qualifying child cannot provide over | Claiming taxpayer must provide over |

| Test | Qualifying Child (QC) | Qualifying Relative (QR) |
|---|---|---|
| | half of his or her own support. | half of the qualifying relative's support. |
| Other | Does not apply | Qualifying relative cannot be a qualifying child of any other taxpayer. |

## Gross Income

The gross income of a qualifying relative dependent must be less than the amount of annual exemption amount.[126] Gross income is all income in the form of property, money, and for services not income tax exempt. Gross income is determined in the following manner:

| Type of income | Gross Income Determination |
|---|---|
| Manufacturing, merchandising, and mining business | Net sales less cost of goods sold, plus miscellaneous business income |
| Rental income | Gross receipts with no reduction for expenses; not net rental income |
| Service business income | Gross income equals gross receipts-no reduction for any expenses. |
| Unemployment compensation | All unemployment is included in gross income |
| Scholarships | Included in gross income to the extent scholarships are taxable |
| Partnership income | Partner's share of gross (not a share of net) partnership income |

---

[126] IRC Sec. 152(d)(1)(B).

| Type of income | Gross Income Determination |
|---|---|
| Community income | Allocated equally between husband and wife.[127] If share exceeds the gross income ceiling, the gross income test is not satisfied, and the person is not a qualifying relative. |
| Social security benefits | Included only if includible in gross income under IRC Sec. 86(a) |
| Sale of property | Gain on sale of property, not total selling price |
| Sheltered workshop income for permanently and totally disabled individuals | Not included as gross income if the main reason for attending is the availability of medical care at the workshop. Income must come solely from workshop activities incidental to the medical care. |

A taxpayer claiming a qualifying relative as a dependent must prove such person's gross income does not exceed the exemption amount.[128] A dependency exemption will be disallowed if a taxpayer cannot prove a qualifying relative's gross income is below the gross income threshold.[129] Moreover, a claimant taxpayer must prove the gross income was less than the threshold amount for the entire year—gross income for

---

[127] Rev. Rul. 54-567, 1954-2 CB 108.

[128] *Rensler v. Comr.*, 9 T.C.M 12, 13 (1950). This case was decided before 2005 when the qualifying relative concept was enacted; however, it would probably apply today.

[129] *Alo v. Commissioner*, 35 T.C.M. 1795, 1798 (1976) and *Counts v. Commissioner*, 42 T.C 755, 761 (1964).

a portion of a tax year less than the threshold amount will not suffice.[130]

> **Observation:** The gross income test only applies to a qualifying relative. It does not apply to a qualifying child if the child satisfies the previously discussed qualifying child tests. If a potential dependent fails any one of the qualifying child tests, then he or she may be claimed as a qualifying relative dependent if all QR tests are satisfied.

> **Observation:** The gross income test is strictly applied. Internal Revenue Code Sec. 152(d)(1)(B) states, "gross income for the calendar year in which such taxable year begins is less than the exemption amount (as defined in section 151(d))." The key point is total gross income cannot be equal to the exemption amount ($3,950 for 2014; $4,000 for 2015; $4,050 for 2016 and 2017) but must be less than the exemption amount.[131]

---

[130] *Ala'ilima v. Commissioner*, 20 T.C.M. 1096, 1098 (1961).

[131] *Carito, Filomena*, 54 TC 1614 (1970). This case was decided prior to 2005, before the qualifying relative concept was created. However, a gross income test existed for years prior to 2005 if a   dependent was over age 18 and not under age 24 and a full-time student. In this case, the potential non-qualifying child dependent had total gross income of

**Example 5-14:** T supports his two single brothers, B1 and B2 for the 2014 calendar year. B1 sells fruit for his only source of income for the year. B1's total sales were $7,000 for fruit that cost $4,000. B2's only source of income is from a rental property that resulted in gross receipts of $4,500 for the entire year. Rental expenses amounted to $1,500. B1 and B2 each earned a net income of $3,000. B1 meets the gross income test, since the gross income test allows the offset of the cost of the fruit sold resulting in B1 having gross income of $3,000. B2 does not meet the gross income test, as the gross income test does not allow offset of rental expenses from gross income in applying the test. B2 has gross income for purposes of this test of $4,500. T can claim B1 as a dependency exemption if all the other qualifying

---

exactly $600 for the year, which was the exemption amount for the 1965 taxable year at issue in the case. The potential dependent had $8 withheld from one of her monthly checks for a death benefit assessment, which would have reduced her gross income below $600 and allowed satisfaction of the gross income test. However, the Tax Court did not allow this offset so the dependency exemption was denied.

relative tests are satisfied. He cannot claim B2.[132]

## Support

The support test applies differently to a qualifying child than to a qualifying relative. A qualifying child may not be self-supporting, that is, he or she cannot provide more than one-half of his or her own support.[133]

In order to meet the support test for a qualifying relative, the claimant taxpayer must provide more than half of a dependent's total support.[134] The total support provided by all others on behalf of the dependent and the amount provided by the dependent must be considered. Only the funds actually spent are considered; income and funds available to a dependent for spending are not considered if they are not spent for support.[135]

---

[132] Cost of goods sold can be deducted in determining gross income if the person is in the manufacturing, merchandising, or mining business (*Hahn v. Comm.*, 30 T.C. 195 (1958), aff'd. per curiam, 271 F.2d 739, 5th Cir., 1959). Gross income is determined without deductions for depreciation (*Cohen v. Comm.*, 12 T.C.M 1065 (1953).

[133] IRC Sec. 152(c)(1)(D).

[134] IRC Sec. 152(d)(1)(C).

[135] IRS Pub. 17 (2016), p 34.

When only the claimant taxpayer and the dependent are involved in supporting the dependent, the claimant taxpayer has to provide over half of the dependent's support. The following discussion will discuss items of support, who provides support, and application of the test when only two individuals are involved; a later discussion will discuss situations where two or more individuals, other than the dependent, called a multiple support agreement, contribute to the dependent's support, but no one provides over half of the dependent's support.

# Types of Support

| Support Source Item | Claimant Taxpayer Provided | Dependent Provided |
|---|---|---|
| 1. Child's wages used for support | No | Yes |
| 2. Child's wages paid by claimant taxpayer | No | Yes |
| 3. Dependent's own funds | No | Yes, if actually spent for support. |
| 4. Tax exempt income: | | |
| 4a. Social Security benefits | Yes, if provided by claimant | Yes, if provided by dependent |
| 4b.Tax-exempt income | Yes, if provided by claimant | Yes, if provided by dependent |
| 4c. Life insurance proceeds | Yes, if provided by claimant | Yes, if provided by dependent |
| 4d. Armed forces family allotments | Yes | Usually provided by claimant |
| 4e. Funds from savings | Yes, if provided by claimant | Yes, if provided by dependent |
| 4f. Loans for college expenses | Yes, if used to pay dependent's college expenses. | Yes, if dependent is primary responsible for the loan |
| 4g. Welfare or food stamps-see below | No-see below | No-see below |
| 5. Foster care expenses: | | |
| 5a. Support payments provided by child placement agency, state or county-see below | No-see below | No-see below |
| 5b. Unreimbursed out-of-pocket expenses for individual not in | Yes, if such expenses are not deductible as a charitable contribution to a | No |

| Support Source Item | Claimant Taxpayer Provided | Dependent Provided |
|---|---|---|
| foster care trade or business-see below | qualified organization. | |
| 5c. Unreimbursed out-of-pocket expenses for individual in a foster care trade or business-see below | Unreimbursed expenses are not considered support provided by claimant. | No |
| 6. Qualified student scholarships-see below | Not considered in the test if dependent is a child of the taxpayer and child is a full-time student | Not considered in the test if dependent is a child of the taxpayer and the child is a full-time student. |
| 7. Medical insurance premiums, including Medicare supplement | Yes, if provided by claimant | Yes, if provided by dependent |
| 7a. Medical insurance benefits, including Medicare | Not considered part of support | Not considered part of support |
| 8. G.I. Bill benefits-see below | No | Yes, counted as support provided by recipient |
| 9. Child care expenses | Yes, even if claimant claims them for a child and dependent care credit | Not applicable |
| 10. Lump-sum advance payment to home for aged-see below | Counted as support provided by the payer-see below | |
| 11. Value of services provided by claiming taxpayer-see below | Not counted as support | Not applicable |
| 11. Lodging | See discussion below | See discussion below |
| 12. Property | See discussion below | See discussion below |

**References are to Support Source Table Items Shown Above:**

**Items 1 and 2**. IRS Pub 17 (2016), p 34.

**Item 3**. Dependent's own earnings or savings not spent for support are not counted in the support test. Id. P 34.

**Items 4a, 4b, 4c, 4d, 4e, and 4f.** Id., p 34.

**Item 4g**. Id., p 34. Benefits provided to a needy person by the state are considered as support provided by the state, unless it is shown that part of such payments are not used for support purposes. NOTE: Support provided by a government may prevent a claimant taxpayer from exceeding the 50% support test and not being able to claim the dependent as a qualifying relative.

**Item 5a**. Id., p 34. Foster care payments from a child placement agency or state/county are considered provided by the source provider, and not provided by the claimant taxpayer or dependent. They may prevent the claimant taxpayer from exceeding the over half support test, as described in Note above.

**Items 5b. and 5c**. Id., ps. 29, 31, and 34.

**Item 6**. See IRC Sec. 152(f)(5). Qualified scholarships are for fees, books, supplies, and equipment for a full-time student. Scholarships for room and board and for other nonqualified items would be taxable income to the recipient and be considered support provided by the recipient.

**Items 7 and 7b**. Id., Pub 17 (2016), p 35.

**Item 8**. Id., p 35. G.I. Bill benefits are not considered scholarships. See Reg. Sec. 1.152-1(c).

**Item 9**. Id., p 35.

**Item 10**. A lump-sum advance payment paid to a home for the aged to care for a dependent relative's life time care is counted as annual support provided by the payer based on the dependent's life expectancy divided into the lump-sum price[136].

> **Example 5-15:** Jim and Jane Smith paid $200,000 to Brown Senior Care Manor to care for Jane's father for his remaining lifetime. If Jane's father has a life expectancy of 21.5 years, Jim and Jane can count $9,302 ($200,000 ÷ 21.5) per year in calculating the support they provide for Jane's father.

**Item 11**. Value of services requiring no specialized training such as child or invalid care and household chores are not considered support. See *Lolita Mosher*, T.C.M. 1970-56; *Mildred Bartsch*, (1964) 41 T.C. 883, and *Frank Markarian v. Commissioner*, (1965, CA-7), 16 AFTR 2d 5785, 17 AFTR 2d 1,352 F2d 870, 65-2

---

[136] Id. p 34.

USTC Par. 9699, 65-2 USTC Para 9755, cert den.
(1966) 384 US 988, affg. (1964) 42 T.C. 640. See
*Lolita Mosher*, T.C.M. 1970-56 and cases cited
therein.

Support items are counted in the year paid, not in a later
year when repaid if they were originally borrowed.[137]
Claimant taxpayers reporting on a fiscal year basis
must provide more than half of a dependent's support
for the calendar year in which the taxpayer's fiscal year
begins.[138]

## Support-Lodging

Lodging for a dependent can be a major support
component that must be considered when determining
if the claimant contributed over half of the support. The
fair rental value of a room, apartment, house, or other
residence in which the dependent resides must be
considered. The fair rental value also includes a
reasonable allowance for the use of furniture and
appliances, plus heat and utilities.[139] Fair rental value,
the amount one could expect to receive in an arm
length's transaction, is used for this test, instead of
actual expenses such as taxes, interest, maintenance,
utilities, cost of appliances and furniture, and other
actual household costs incurred. The claimant can
claim the entire lodging amount if he or she provides
the total lodging, based on the value described above.

---

[137] Id. p 34.

[138] Id. p 34.

[139] Id. p 35.

If the claimant and the dependent share the lodgings' cost, the cost must be divided between the two parties.[140]

A potential dependent who lives in his or her own home counts the entire fair rental value of the lodging as his or her contribution. A potential dependent living in lodging rent-free must reduce his or her lodging share by the fair rental value of the free lodging.[141]

## Support-Capital Expenditures

Capital items are measured at fair market value; a value the property would sell for in an arm's length transaction. Generally, a capital expenditure such as a TV purchased for a dependent for exclusive use of the dependent counts as support provided by the buyer.[142] A capital item, such as a lawn mower purchased for a dependent who then had lawn mowing responsibilities, is not considered support provided for the dependent, as it benefited all the household residents.[143]

An automobile purchased by a claimant taxpayer registered in the claimant's name, not exclusively used by a dependent, cannot be counted as claimant provided support. Any out-of-pocket expenses paid by the claimant can be counted as the claimant's

---

[140] Id. p 35.

[141] Id. p 35.

[142] Id. p 35, Example 2.

[143] Id. p 35, Example 1.

support.[144] An automobile purchased by a dependent with dependent's own funds is considered support provided by the dependent.[145]


## Support Test Application

**Example 5-16:** Bill and Cathy Smith, their two children, and Cathy's parents (Jack and Jane) all live in Bill and Cathy's home. Jack has a nontaxable pension of $4,200, which is spent equally for Jack and Jane's support of clothing, recreation, etc. Total food expense of the household is $6,000 for six household members. The fair rental value of Jack and Jane's lodging is $1,000 each, which includes utilities and heat and all furniture and appliances. Jane had medical bills of $600 paid by Bill and Cathy.[146]

The following table summarizes the support provided by each:

---

[144] Id. p 35, Example 3.

[145] Id. p 35, Example 4.

[146] Based on IRS Pub 17 (2016), p 34, Example 2.

| Support Provided | Jack's Expense | Jane's Expense | Bill and Cathy's Share for: | |
|---|---|---|---|---|
| | | | Father | Mother |
| Fair rental value | $1,000 | $1,000 | $1,000 | $1,000 |
| Pension support | 2,100 | 2,100 | | |
| Share of food | 1,000 | 1,000 | 1,000 | 1,000 |
| Mother's medical | | 600 | | 600 |
| Total | $4,100 | $4,700 | $2,000 | $2,600 |

Total support provided by Bill and Cathy: $2,600 + $2,000 = $4,600

Total support for Jack and Jane: $4,100 + $4,700 = $8,800

> **Observation 1:** If the support test was applied to both parents at the same time, Bill and Cathy would meet the over half support test, as they provided over half the support, contributing over 52% ($4,600 ÷ $8,800) of both parents combined. However, the support test is applied separately for each parent.[147]

> **Observation 2:** When the support test is applied to Jack and Jane separately, Bill and Cathy did not provide over half of Jack's support, as $2,000 ÷ $4,100 is

---

[147] IRS Pub 17 (2016), p 4. Also, see Rev. Rul. 72-591, 1972-2 C.B. 84.

less than half. Jane's support provided by Bill and Cathy is over half, as $2,600 ÷ $4,700 is over 55%. Overall, Bill and Cathy satisfy the support test for Jane, but not for Jack.

**Observation 3:** When one or more potential dependents may qualify as dependents, it is crucial the support tests and other tests be reviewed in year-end planning to satisfy all tests before the year closes. A support test below half could be increased to over half by a support item expenditure before year-end.

**Observation 4:** In the above situation, the fair rental value of lodging was given as $1,000 each for Jack and Jane. In situations where the dependent parents live with the claimant taxpayer, the fair rental value must be divided equally among all household members if they have free access to the entire home.[148] If Jack and Jill would have occupied the residence for less than a full twelve months, which was not considered a temporary absence, the support amount would consist of actual

---

[148] *Daya, Gabriel M.*, T.C.M. 2000-360.

months of occupancy.[149] Fair rental value would be calculated based on the previous discussion.

## Proof of Support

The support test is an annual test, and previous years support amounts do not count in subsequent years.[150] Taxpayer claimants have the burden that they provided over half the support of a qualifying relative dependent.[151] Claimant taxpayers must show their support contribution and total support for the dependent.[152] Failing to provide evidence of the dependent's total support will result in denial of the dependency exemption, as the over half test cannot be calculated.[153] Evidence of total support will not be necessary if a claimant can prove that he or she is the only person providing support.[154] Where the dependent has earnings, the claimant will have to establish what amount each contributes to support.[155]

---

[149] *Muracca, Francis*, T.C.M. 1984-234.

[150] *McDevitt*, 13 T.C.M. (CCH) 193 (1954).

[151] *Rinaldo v. Commissioner*, 36 T.C.M. (CCH) 483 (1977).

[152] *Schmidt*, T.C.M. 1991-587.

[153] *Cherry*, T.C.M. 1998-360 and *Bernardo*, T.C.M. 2004-199.

[154] Id., *Schmidt*.

[155] See *Beard*, T.C.M. 1998-110 and *Sumner*, 13 T.C.M. (CCH) 140.

The claimant's evidence must support the genuineness of the claim for the support provided.[156]

## Multiple Support Agreements

A situation may arise when one person does not provide over half of a dependent's support, but two or more persons provide it, where each satisfy all the qualifying relative tests except for the support test. In this case, one individual in the group who provides more than 10% of a dependent's support and meets all the other qualifying relative tests can take the dependency exemption. Each individual who provides more than 10% of the dependent's support and does not claim the dependency exemption must sign Form 2120, Multiple Support Declaration, agreeing not to claim the dependency exemption. The individual claiming the dependency exemption must attach the completed Form 2120 to his or her income tax return.

A multiple support agreement exemption can be claimed for a dependent related to the claimant or for someone who lived with the claimant all year as a member of the claimant's household. A dependency exemption claimed using a multiple support agreement does not qualify the taxpayer for head-of-household filing status.[157]

A multiple support agreement applies to a qualifying relative dependent and does not apply to a qualifying

---

[156] Rev. Rul. 72-591, 1972-2 C.B. 84.

[157] IRC Sec. 2 (b)(3)(B)(ii).

child. This is because the support test for a qualifying child applies only if the child provides more than half of his or her own support, the multiple support rules do not apply to them.[158]

> **Example 5-17:** Dan, his sister, and two brothers provide the total support for their mother. Dan provides 45%, his sister provides 35%, while the two remaining brothers each provide 10%. Dan and his sister provide a combined 80% of the mother's support. Dan or his sister can claim the mother's dependency exemption. If Dan takes the dependency exemption, his sister must sign Form 2120 not to take an exemption for her mother. The other two brothers each provide only 10% of the support; neither can take the exemption, and do not have to sign Form 2120, as they did not contribute over 10% of the support.[159]

> **Example 5-18:** Assume Dan and his sister each provide 20% of their mother's support. The other two brothers provide nothing. The remaining 60% of the mother's support is provided equally by unrelated

---

[158] Conf. Rept. No 108-696 (PL 108-311), p 63-64.

[159] IRS Pub 17 (2016), p 35, Example 1.

individuals. The mother did not live with any of her relatives. As over half of the mother's support is provided by individuals who cannot claim an exemption for her, no one can take her exemption.[160]

**Observation:** The individuals meeting all the tests for a dependency exemption, except for the over one-half support test, must contribute over 50% of the total support to qualify for a multiple support agreement. If three sisters each contribute one-third of their mother's total support, each of them is entitled to claim their mother's dependency exemption. Only one sister may claim the exemption, while the other two must sign Form 2120 agreeing not to claim the exemption. The sister claiming the exemption must attach Form 2120 to her tax return.

---

[160] Id., Example 2.

## Items Not Included in Support

The following items are not included in total support[161]:

- Federal, state, and local income taxes paid from a dependent's own funds
- Social Security and Medicare taxes paid from dependent's own funds
- Life insurance premiums
- Funeral expenses
- Scholarships received by claimant's child if the child is a full-time student and
- Survivors' and Dependents' Educational Assistance payments used for the support of the claimant's child who receives them.

## Effect of Proposed Regulations

The proposed regulations make extensive changes to existing Sec. 152 regulations   to update them for WFTRA changes passed in 2004 and incorporate the WFTRA provisions.   Readers are directed to read the proposed regulations for specific issues.   Limited highlights will be shown here. The general rules section for dependents in the proposed regulations discuss:

1. Qualifying relative relationship
2. Gross income test
3. Qualifying relative support test

---

[161] Id., p 35.

4. Not a qualifying child test including illustrative examples of this situation

## Chapter 6

## Child Tax Credit

The child tax credit was originally enacted in The Taxpayer Relief Act of 1997 (P.L. 105-34) as a $500 nonrefundable credit. The Economic Growth and Tax Relief Reconciliation Act of 2001 (EGTRRA; P.L. 107-16) raised the credit to $1,000 and made the credit refundable for taxpayers having more than $10,000 (adjusted for inflation) of earned income. The American Recovery and Reinvestment Act of 2009 (ARRA: P.L. 111-5) reduced the $10,000 to $3,000 (not adjusted for inflation).

The Tax Relief, Unemployment Insurance Reauthorization, and Job Creation Act of 2010 (P.L. 111-312) extended the EGTRRA and ARRA changes through 2012. At the end of 2012, the changes of a $1,000 child tax credit and the $10,000 threshold for refundable credit were made permanent. The American Taxpayer Relief Act (ATRA; P.L. 112-240) extended the reduced $10,000 threshold to $3,000 through 2017.

The Protecting Americans from Tax Hikes Act of 2015 (PATH Act, signed on December 18, 2015) reduced the $10,000 earned income limit that was supposed to take effect in 2018 to a permanent amount of $3,000 not adjusted for inflation.

The child tax credit is an annual $1,000 tax credit available with respect to taxpayer's qualifying children under age 17. It consists of a nonrefundable portion and a refundable portion, called the additional child tax credit. This credit should not be confused with the child and dependent credit that will be discussed later. The specific requirements and application of the child tax credit will be presented in the following discussion.

**Child Tax Credit Requirements**

To qualify for the child tax credit, one must have:

- A qualifying child defined in the same manner as it is for claiming a dependency exemption. The child must be a son/daughter, stepchild, foster child, brother/sister, stepbrother/stepsister, or a descendant of any of them.
- The qualifying child is a U.S. citizen, a U.S. national, or a resident alien of the United States.[162]
    - The qualifying child for the child tax credit does not include a child who is a resident of a country contiguous to the United States. This requirement excludes a child

---

[162] IRC Sec. 24 (c)(2) applies Sec. 152(b)(3)(A) wording without the phrase, ..." or a country contiguous to the United States". This limits a dependent for the child tax credit to a citizen, national, or resident alien of the U.S. This application excludes a child who lives in Mexico or Canada. Also, a child living in Mexico or Canada could qualify for a dependency exemption, but not be a dependent for the child tax credit.

who lives in Mexico or Canada when such child could be a qualifying child for dependency exemption purposes.

- Adopted children are always treated as a taxpayer's own children. Adopted children include children lawfully placed with the claiming taxpayer for legal adoption. For adopted children who are not a U.S. citizen, U.S. national, or U.S. resident, refer to the Citizenship discussion in Chapter 2, Dependency Exemptions Requirements for both Qualifying Children and Qualifying Relatives.

- The qualifying child must be under age 17 at the end of the tax year, December 31, for a calendar year tax year.
- The qualifying child was not self-supporting for the credit year.
- The qualifying child must live with the claiming taxpayer for more than half the tax year
    - Temporary absences for school, vacations, business, medical care, and juvenile facility detention count as time lived with the claiming taxpayer.
- The qualifying child qualifies as a dependent on the claiming taxpayer's tax return.

- The qualifying child's name and social security number or taxpayer identification number must appear on the return.
- The qualifying child did not file a joint return for the year, or it is filed to claim a refund of withheld income tax or estimated tax paid.

**Example 6-1:** Assume a taxpayer's dependent turns age 17 on December 31, 2014, the last day of the tax year. Because he turned age 17 during the 2014 tax year, he is ineligible for the child tax credit, as the requirement is under age 17 at the end of the tax year. [163]

**Example 6-2:** In order to claim the child tax credit, the claiming taxpayer must claim the qualifying child as a dependency exemption. In situations where the qualifying child meets all the child tax credit requirements and the parents are divorced, separated, or never married, and the custodial parent provides a properly completed Form 8332 allowing the noncustodial parent to claim a dependency exemption for

---

[163] Rev. Rul. 2003-72, 2003-33 IRB 346.

the child, the noncustodial parent is also entitled to the child tax credit.[164]

## Credit Amount and Limitations

The child tax credit is subject to two limitations. The first limitation reduces the benefit for higher incomes and is based on modified adjusted gross income. The second limitation limits the amount of all nonrefundable personal tax credits (including the child tax credit) to the sum of the regular income tax reduced by the foreign tax credit plus the alternative minimum tax. Each limitation will be discussed separately. The excess advance premium tax credit repayment is considered a chapter 1 tax, discussed later.[165]

## Modified Adjusted Gross Income (MAGI) Phase-out

The MAGI phase-out starts when MAGI exceeds the lower amount shown in the table and has a length dependent on the number of qualifying children:

---

[164] IRS Notice 2006-86, 2006-2 C.B. 680. (Notice 2006-86 will be obsolete by the proposed regulations.) See Proposed Regulations 1.152-2(g)(3) and (4).

[165] IRC Sec. 36B(f)(2)(A).

| Filing Status | Modified Adjusted Gross Income (MAGI) | One Qualifying Child | Two Qualifying Children | Three Qualifying Children |
|---|---|---|---|---|
| Married filing jointly | $110,000 | $110,001-129,001 | $110,001-$149,001 | $110,001-$169,001 |
| An unmarried individual [a] | 75,000 | $75,001-94,001 | $75,001-114,001 | $75,001-134,001 |
| Married filing separately | 55,000 | $55,001-74,001 | $55,001-94,001 | $55,001-114,001 |

[a] Single, head of household, or qualifying widow(er) filing status.

> **Observation:** The threshold phase-out amounts in the above table are not inflation adjusted.[166] The amounts in the above table will stay the same in subsequent years. As a result, taxpayers with MAGI in the phase-out range will lose more child tax credit as yearly income increases.

> **Observation:** Note, a qualifying widow(er) is entitled to use the married filing jointly tax rate schedule or tax tables to calculate the income tax for

---

[166] IRC Sec. 24(b) and House Report 105-148 (PL 105-34), p 310.

two years after the year of the spouse's death, assuming all conditions for those two years are satisfied. A qualifying widow(er) would have to use the $110,000 MAGI exclusion in the year of the spouse's death if the surviving spouse can file as married filing jointly. The surviving spouse would use the lower unmarried individual $75,000 MAGI exclusion for the two years after the year of the spouse's death, if he or she qualifies for this filing status.[167]

Modified adjusted gross income is calculated as follows:

- Adjusted gross income (AGI), adding back the following amounts:
- Any income excluded related to a Puerto Rican income exclusion, (IRC Sec. 933)
- Any foreign income and foreign housing expenses excluded shown on Form 2555 or Form 2555-EZ
- Any income excluded from sources within American Samoa, Guam, and Northern Mariana Islands. (IRC Sec. 931).

---

[167] IRS Pub 972 (2016), p 3 and IRC Sec. 24(b)(2)(B). Publication 972 specifically lists qualifying widow(er) in the same category as single and head of household filing status.

If taxpayers do not have any of these add-back amounts on their tax return, modified AGI and AGI are equal.

>**Example 6-3:** John and Mary have one qualifying child who meets all the requirements for the child tax credit. They have AGI of $125,000 and no add-back amounts in arriving at MAGI. Based on a married filing jointly tax return filing status, John and Mary are $15,000 into the phase-out range. The child tax credit is reduced $50 for each $1,000, or fraction thereof, that MAGI exceeds the start of the phase-out range. This results in a reduction of $50 times 15, the number of thousands John and Mary are within the phase-out range, a reduction of $750 for a remaining $250 of child tax credit that is available to the taxpayers. If they had two qualifying children, they would have $1,250 of credit available as a nonrefundable credit before considering the nonrefundable credit limitation.
>
>**Observation:** The length of the MAGI phase-out range depends on taxpayer's filing status and number of qualifying children. The phase-out range for John and Mary with one qualifying child starts at $110,001 and when MAGI exceeds $129,000 by one dollar, the $1,000 credit is fully phased-out. For

two qualifying children and married filing joint, the phase-out range starts $110,001 and phases out the $2,000 of credit when MAGI exceeds $149,000 by one dollar. Head of household, single filers or qualifying widow(er) with one qualifying child have a phase-out range equal to MAGI of $75,001 to $94,001. Married filing separately with one qualifying child has a phase-out range equal to MAGI of $55,001 to $74,001. Refer to the above table for the phase-out ranges.

**Observation:** Note the phase-out rule is written "for each $1,000, or fraction thereof," that MAGI exceeds the start of the phase-out level. Therefore, if John and Mary's MAGI was $125,001, or one-dollar more, they would lose another $50 of child tax credit.

**Example 6-4:** Assume Mary is a qualifying widower (surviving spouse) in the year after John's death with two children who both meet the child tax credit requirements and has a $95,000 MAGI. As a qualifying widower, her MAGI phase-out range begins at $75,001; a lot lower than the married filing jointly phase-out range. Mary would have $2,000 of child tax credit before any reduction. The MAGI reduction would reduce the $2,000 by $1,000, leaving her with $1,000 of child tax credit before the considering the nonrefundable credit limitation. The child tax credit is reduced by one-half, as she is at the mid-point of the phase-out range with a $95,000 MAGI.

## Tax Liability Limitation

The child tax credit contains nonrefundable and refundable portions. The refundable portion is referred to as the additional child tax credit. The additional child tax credit applies to all or part of the credit not used as a nonrefundable credit.

The maximum credit is $1,000 for each qualifying child. The entire credit of $1,000 (assuming only one qualifying child) can be used to offset the sum of the regular income tax reduced by the foreign tax credit plus the alternative minimum tax and excess advance premium tax credit repayment.

**Example 6-5:** Assume the claiming taxpayer has $1,500 of regular income tax reduced by the foreign tax credit plus alternative minimum tax. The $1,000 of child tax credit, the only nonrefundable personal credit available to taxpayer in this example, will reduce the $1,500, leaving $500 as a remaining balance.

**Example 6-6:** Assume the claiming taxpayer has only $750 shown as regular income tax reduced by foreign tax credit and no alternative minimum tax, resulting in $750 of the $1,000 child tax credit to offset the regular income tax liability. The $250 nonrefundable amount of the credit may qualify as refundable, additional child tax credit, discussed later.

**Observation:** The sum of the regular income tax, the alternative minimum tax, and the excess advance premium tax credit repayment is line 47 of Form 1040 for 2016. Nonrefundable tax credits offset line 47 based on the priority shown on the child tax credit worksheet and expressed in the footnote.[168] Many nonrefundable tax

---

[168] IRC Sec. 26(a). For tax years beginning after December 31, 2011, all nonrefundable personal tax credits are allowed to the full extent of the taxpayer's regular income tax liability (including excess advance premium credit repayments), reduced by the foreign tax credit, plus the alternative minimum tax. Special calculations are necessary to determine the amount of the nonrefundable child tax credit when other nonrefundable credits are present. The starting point is the regular income tax plus the alternative minimum tax plus excess advance premium tax credit repayments. Line 47 on a 2016 Form 1040 includes the regular income tax, alternative minimum tax, and excess advance premium tax credit repayment. The

credits offset the Line 47 total, the
foreign tax credit being the first one.
The child tax credit offsets the Line 47
amount as described in the footnote.

Any child tax credit not claimed as a nonrefundable
credit may qualify as additional child tax credit. The
additional child tax credit, being refundable, will be

---

sum of the following credits are subtracted from the Line
47 (2016 Form 1040) total in the following order: (1)
foreign tax credit; (2) child and dependent care credit; (3)
education credits; (4) retirement savings credit; (5)
nonbusiness energy property credit (Form 5695, Part II,
Line 30); (6) personal use alternative motor vehicle credit
(Form 8910, Part III, Line 15; (7) personal use of qualified
plug-in electric drive motor vehicle credit, Form 8936, Part
III, Line 23; and (8) credit for the elderly and disabled,
Schedule R, Line 22.

In addition, credits claimed for (a) mortgage interest credit,
Form 8396; (b) adoption credit, Form 8839; (c) residential
energy efficient property credit (Form 5695, Part I); and
(d) District of Columbia first-time homebuyer credit, Form
8859; are also subtracted from the Line 47 total. The sum
of these credits, in both these categories, reduces the Line
47 total to the amount of nonrefundable child credit that
can be claimed. If any of these credits are present, a lower
amount of nonrefundable child tax credit can be claimed
on 2016 Form 1040 Line 52, increasing the potential
amount of refundable child tax credit that can be claimed.
(See 2016 Form 1040 Instructions, Form 1040 Child Tax
Credit Worksheets, noting when the Child Tax Credit
Worksheet in IRS Pub 972 (2016), pgs., 5-10, must be
used instead of the worksheet in the Form 1040
instructions in certain circumstances.)

shown in the payments section of Form 1040 and treated just like withheld income taxes.

For taxpayers with no more than two qualifying children, the refundable child tax credit is equal to the lesser of the unclaimed portion of the nonrefundable credit amount or 15 percent of a taxpayer's earned income in excess of $3,000.[169] Taxpayers with less than $3,000 of earned income will not qualify to use this method to calculate the refundable portion of the child tax credit. Taxpayers with one or two qualifying children and $3,000 or less in earned income will not qualify for any refundable child tax credit. Taxpayers with three or more qualifying children determine their refundable child tax credit limited to the lesser of

- The unclaimed portion of the nonrefundable child tax credit [170]
- The amount calculated using the no more than two qualifying children method mentioned above [171]
- The excess of the taxpayer's share of Social Security taxes (including one-half of the self-employment taxes) over taxpayer's earned income credit for the tax year. Taxpayers with one or two qualifying children cannot use this method. [172]

---

[169] IRC Sec. 24(d)(1)(B)(i).

[170] IRC Sec. 24(d)(1)(A).

[171] IRC Sec. 24(d)(1)(B)(i).

[172] IRC Sec. 24(d)(1)(B)(ii).

**Example 6-7:** Assume a taxpayer had $250 of nonrefundable child tax credit from Example 6-6 that can be considered for additional child tax credit. If all of the AGI is earned income, the calculation for the additional child tax credit is:

| | |
|---|---|
| Earned income | $20,000 |
| Less: base amount | 3,000 |
| Remaining amount | 17,000 |
| Percentage of remaining amount | 15% |
| Calculated amount | 2,550 |
| Additional child tax credit-limited to $250 or $2,550 | $250 |

**Observation:** Taxpayers with one or two qualifying children and $3,000 or less in earned income will not qualify for the 15% of earned income in excess $3,000 calculation to convert nonrefundable child tax credit to refundable, additional child tax credit. As a result, the nonrefundable child tax credit will be lost. As previously discussed, the $3,000 amount in this calculation is fixed, and not adjusted for inflation, and was made permanent by the PATH Act previously discussed.

**Planning Pointer:** Refer to Optional Method for Social Security Coverage in chapter 8 discussing use of this optional method to qualify for or increase amounts for the earned income tax credit, the refundable child tax credit, and child and dependent care credit.

## Other Aspects

Except in cases where the taxable year is closed by a taxpayer's death, the child tax credit is allowed for tax years consisting of 12 months.[173] Military families with combat zone pay excludable from AGI can elect to include the excluded combat pay as earned income for the additional child tax credit calculation.[174]

Paid preparers must comply with due diligence requirements for refundable tax credits for earned income tax credit, child tax credit, and American Opportunity Tax Credit. (IRS Pub. 4687, Revised 8-2016 and T. D. 9799, December 2, 2016, Federal Register, Volume 81, Number 233, Monday, December 5, 2016)

The Bipartisan Congressional Trade Priorities and Accountability Act of 2015 (HR 2146) and Trade Preferences Extension Act (HR 1245) limits the child tax credit for taxpayers who elect to exclude any amount of foreign earned income or housing costs. These taxpayers are not able to claim the refundable portion of the child tax credit for the tax year. This

---

[173] IRC Sec. 24(f).

[174] IRC Sec. 24(d)(1).

change is effective for tax years beginning after December 31, 2014.[175].

The name and taxpayer identification number of a qualifying child eligible for the child tax credit must be provided on the tax return for the taxable year and that taxpayer identification number must have been issued on or before the due date for filing such return.[176]

No child tax credit will be allowed if the identifying number of the taxpayer claiming the child tax credit was issued after the due date for filing the return for the taxable year.[177]

No child tax credit is allowed for any taxable year in the disallowance period. The disallowance period is 10 taxable years after the most recent taxable year for which there is a final determination the taxpayer's claim for the credit was due to fraud (2 years if due to reckless or intentional disregard of rules and regulations, but not due to fraud).[178]

**2017 Disaster Tax Relief**

See the discussion at the end chapter on Earned Income Tax Credit under the Disaster Tax Relief headnote.

---

[175] Sec. 24(d)(5).

[176] Sec. 24(e)(1).

[177] Sec. 24(e)(2).

[178] Sec. 24(g).

## Chapter 7

## Child and Dependent Care Credit

Sec. 21 provides a nonrefundable credit for individuals who have one or more qualifying individuals who incur employment-related expenses enabling them to be gainfully employed. This chapter will discuss the requirements to claim this credit.

### Qualifying Individual

Qualifying individuals are:

a. a taxpayer's under age 13 dependent defined in Sec. 152(a)(1) as defined for dependency purposes,[179]

b. a taxpayer's dependent who is physically and mentally incapable of self-care (as defined in Sec. 152) who resides with the taxpayer for more than half the tax year. For this purpose, the gross income test for qualifying relatives, the rule a joint filer cannot be a dependent, and the rule a dependent cannot have dependents do not apply.[180]

c. a taxpayer's spouse who is physically or mentally incapable of self-care who resides with taxpayer in the same place of abode for more than half the tax year.[181]

---

[179] IRC Sec. 21(b)(1)(A).

[180] IRC Sec. 21(b)(1)(B).

[181] IRC Sec. 21(b)(1)(C).

**Observation:** Each of the three qualifying individual categories listed above must have the same principal place of abode as the taxpayer for over half the tax year. Qualifying individuals under age 13 are required to do so based on the Sec. 152(a)(1) requirements, while categories b. and c., above, are required by the requirements in Sec. 21(b)(1)(B) and (C). As discussed later, qualifying individuals in categories b. and c. must also reside with the taxpayer at least 8 hours per day required by Sec. 21(b)(2)(B).

**Observation:** The 8-hour requirement imposed on categories b. and c. qualifying individuals prevents a taxpayer from claiming the child and dependent care credit when the care is provided outside taxpayer's principal place of abode for an entire 24-hour day.

**Observation:** An individual may claim the credit for a qualifying individual who shares the same place of abode for more than half the year even if the claiming individual does not provide more than half the cost of maintaining the household.[182] The same place of

---

[182] Conf. Rept. No. 108-696 (PL 108-311), p 64, relating to the Working Families Tax Relief Act of 2004 removed the requirement that a claiming taxpayer maintain a household for this credit effective with years beginning after December 31, 2004.

abode test is not satisfied if at any time
during the taxable year the relationship
between the qualified individual and the
claiming taxpayer is in violation of
local law.[183]

**Observation:**     Employment-related
expenses incurred in a year when an
under age 13 qualifying individual turns
13, qualify for the credit to the extent
the qualified services are performed
prior to the qualifying individual's 13th
birthday.[184]

### Limitations on and Amount of the Credit

The credit starts at 35% of employment-related
expenses (discussed later) for taxpayers with AGI of
$15,000 or less, declining by 1% for each $2,000
increase in AGI, to 20% regardless of taxpayer's AGI.

The following table presents the credit percentages
decline as AGI increases:

| Adjusted Gross Income | Credit Rate | Maximum Credit | |
|---|---|---|---|
| | | One Child | Two or More Children |
| $15,000 or less | 35% | $1,050 | $2,100 |
| $15,001-17,000 | 34% | $1,020 | $2,040 |
| $17,001-19,000 | 33% | $990 | $1,980 |
| $19,001-21,000 | 32% | $960 | $1,920 |
| $21,001-23,000 | 31% | $930 | $1,860 |
| $23,001-25,000 | 30% | $900 | $1,800 |
| $25,001-27,000 | 29% | $870 | $1,740 |
| $27,001-29,000 | 28% | $840 | $1,680 |
| $29,001-31,000 | 27% | $810 | $1,620 |
| $31,001-33,000 | 26% | $780 | $1,560 |
| $33,001-35,000 | 25% | $750 | $1,500 |

[183] IRC Sec. 21(e)(1).

[184] Reg. Sec. 1.21-1(a)(5), Example 2.

|  |  | Maximum Credit | |
| Adjusted Gross Income | Credit Rate | One Child | Two or More Children |
| --- | --- | --- | --- |
| $35,001-37,000 | 24% | $720 | $1,440 |
| $37,001-39,000 | 23% | $690 | $1,380 |
| $39,001-41,000 | 22% | $660 | $1,320 |
| $41,000-43,000 | 21% | $630 | $1,260 |
| 43,001 and over | 20% | $600 | $1,200 |

Employment-related expenses are limited to $3,000 for one child or $6,000 for two or more children.[185] These maximum amounts are reduced by any amounts excludable under Sec. 129 (dependent care assistance exclusion).[186]

A taxpayer can claim $6,000 maximum amount of employment-related expenses even if they are disproportionate between qualifying individuals. A taxpayer can claim a maximum of $6,000 of employment expenses before any reductions if $4,000 and $2,000 of expenses are incurred for two qualifying individuals.[187]

**Employment-related Expenses**

Employment-related expenses qualifying for the credit are household service expenses or expenses for the care of qualifying individuals that are necessary for the claiming individual's gainful employment. Household services consist of ordinary and necessary services necessary for household maintenance and must be attributable to the qualifying individual's care.[188] This would include household services, such as babysitter,

---

[185] IRC Sec. 21(c).

[186] Ibid.

[187] Reg. Sec. 1-21-2(a)(3).

[188] IRS Letter Ruling 8437055.

house cleaner, and housekeeper costs, necessary for household maintenance provided and are provided, in part, for the qualifying individual's care.

Expenses for the care of the qualifying individual qualify as employment-related expense    if their primary function adds to the qualifying individual's well-being and protection.[189] A provider hired to care for a qualifying individual in the taxpayer's home fits this category. Additional cost of room and board for a caregiver in the home may qualify as household services.[190]    Payroll    taxes    (Social    Security, unemployment, and state payroll and state employment taxes) related to caregiver's employment can be employment-related expenses.[191] Expenses paid for lodging, food, and clothing are basic living expenses and are not for the care of a qualifying individual.[192]

Expenses for pre-school, nursery or related programs for children below kindergarten level are for the care of the qualifying individual and are employment-related expenses; however, expenses for kindergarten or higher education are not employment-related expenses. Before or after school programs for kindergarten or higher education may qualify for employment-related expenses.[193]

---

[189] Reg. Sec. 1.21-1(d)(1).

[190] Reg. Sec. 1.21-1(d)(10) and (d)(12), Example 6.

[191] Reg. Sec. 1.21-1(d)(9).

[192] Reg. Sec. 1.21-1(d)(1).

[193] Reg. Sec. 1.21-1(d)(5).

Expenses paid for day camps[194] qualify while overnight camp[195] expenses do not qualify for employment-related expenses.

Employment-related expenses are eligible for the credit in the latter of (1) the tax year in which the services are incurred or (2) the tax year the expenses are paid regardless of the taxpayer's method of accounting.[196]

Payments for services outside the household count for employment-related expenses only if incurred for (1) a qualifying individual under age 13 or (2) any other qualifying individual (as described in Sec. 21 (b)(1)(B) and (C)) who regularly spends over eight hours of each day in taxpayer's principal place of abode (and is not a dependent under age 13).[197] Payments made to a dependent care center must be a center that complies with all state and local laws and regulations.[198]

> **Observation:** Employment-related expenses which are incurred for services outside the taxpayer's household fall into two categories: (a) the first category is for a qualifying individual under age 13 (Sec. 21 (b)(2)(B)(i) and (b) the second category is for a dependent physically or mentally incapable of self-care or for a spouse physically or mentally incapable

---

[194] Reg. Sec. 1.21-1(d)(7), Example 4.

[195] Reg. Sec. 1.21-1(d)(6).

[196] Reg. Sec. 1.21-1(a)(3).

[197] IRC Sec. 21(b)(2)(B)(i)(ii).

[198] IRC Sec. 21(b)(2)(C).

of self-care ((Sec. 21 (b)(2)(B)(ii). Both of these code sections refer to a qualifying individual defined in Sec. 21(b)(1). Note when a qualifying individual or spouse are both physically or mentally incapable of self-care, they must reside in the taxpayer's household at least 8 hours per day.

**Observation:** This credit is available for 24-hour care outside the taxpayer's household for qualifying individuals (dependents) under age 13 and is not available to the other categories of qualifying individuals.[199] There is no 8-hour-per-day requirement of residing in the taxpayer's household; however, the under age 13 qualifying individual must have the same principal place of abode as the taxpayer for more than half the year, as previously mentioned.

The taxpayer must be gainfully employed for the expenses to qualify. Payments made for days when taxpayer is not working, such as days not worked for a part-time job or missing work for illness (unless temporary, up to two consecutive weeks[200]) are not employment-related expenses. Expenses paid when taxpayer is absent for a four-month illness are not employment-related expenses, even if taxpayer is paid

---

[199] IRC Sec. 21(b)(2)(B)(ii) requiring a qualifying individual not under age 13 to regularly spend at least 8 hours each day in the qualifying individual's household.

[200] Reg. Sec. Sec. 1.21-1(c)(3), Example 4.

by employer's wage continuation plan[201]. Part-time workers who have days off and have to pay for a weekly or longer care rate, with no option to pay a daily care rate, can count the entire week's care and do not have to exclude care paid for days not worked.[202]

Employment-related expenses paid to taxpayer's dependent (as defined in Sec. 152(c)), dependent's spouse, or child of the taxpayer, as defined in Sec. 152(f)(1) under age 19 at the end of the tax year, taxpayer's spouse, or parent of taxpayer's child (who is not the taxpayer's spouse) do not qualify as employment-related expenses.[203]

> **Observation:** The restriction of paying qualified employment expenses to relatives and dependents prevents taking the credit for payments to close family members.

### Earned Income Limit on Employment-Related Expenses

The $3,000 and $6,000 maximum employment-expense related amounts are limited in the following situations:

---

[201] Reg. Sec. 1-21-1(c)(3), Example 3.

[202] Reg. Sec. 1.21-1(c)(2) iii.

[203] IRC Sec. 21(e)(6) and Reg. Sec. 1.21-4(c) Examples 1, 2, and 3.

a.  Limited to earned income (as defined in Sec. 32(c)(2)[204] for an individual who is unmarried at the end of the year.

b.  Limited to the lesser of the individual's or spouse's earned income if married at the end of the year.

In situations where a spouse is a full-time student (five calendar months during the tax year[205]) or a spouse is a qualifying individual incapable of self-care, each is deemed to have earned income of $250 per month for one qualifying individual or $500 per month, if two or more qualifying individuals are present in the household. The deemed earned income rule applies to only one spouse for any given month.[206]

> **Observation:** Only one spouse can use the deemed income rule for a given month. If both spouses were full-time students or one was a student and the other was incapable of self-care, only one can use the deemed monthly amount to calculate earned income for this test. Assuming the couple has no other earned income, the couple would be ineligible for the credit, as the earned income limitation would limit employment expenses to zero for the spouse with no earned income.[207]

---

[204] Reg. Sec. 1.21-2(b)(3).

[205] IRC. Sec. 21(e)(7) and Reg. Sec 1.21-2(b)(4)(ii).

[206] IRC Sec. 21 (d)(1) and (2).

[207] Reg. Sec. 1.21-2(c), Example 3.

**Observation:** A full-time student can use the $250 or $500 deemed earned income (depending on the number of qualifying individuals in the household) amount for every month he or she is a student and count any other earned income for months not in school for total earned income for the tax year.[208]

**Planning Pointer:** Taxpayer(s) can elect to count nontaxable combat pay as earned income to avoid the reduction of employment-related expenses caused by the earned income limitation. This income can be included for purposes of this credit even if it is not included for purposes of the earned income credit or the exclusion or deduction for child and dependent care benefits.[209] Moreover, taxpayers who uses the optional method of computing self-employment net earnings can treat such amount as earned income for the child and dependent care credit.

---

[208] Instructions for Form 2441 (2016), p 4. Reg. Sec. 1.21-2(b)(3) defines earned income for child and dependent care as defined for the earned income credit.

[209] Sec. 32(c)(2)(B)(vi) as earned income for the child and dependent care credit is based on Sec. 32(c)(2) and IRS Pub 503 (2016), p. 4.

## Employment-related Expenses and Employer Provided Dependent Care Assistance

As previously mentioned, employment-related expenses must be reduced by employer provided dependent care assistance (Sec. 129). The amount of these benefits should be reported on Form W-2. A taxpayer receiving $1,500 in benefits from such a plan would have to reduce any employment-related expenses to be gainfully employed by the $1,500 to determine the amount of employment expenses that qualify for the child and dependent care credit.

> **Planning Pointer:** If a taxpayer's employer has a flexible spending account (FSA) where money can be withheld from an employee's earnings for payment of employment-related expenses, the employee/taxpayer must determine if he or she should make a contribution to the FSA, or not make such contribution and claim the child and dependent care credit on their tax return. In general, when taxpayer has a 15% or less marginal tax rate, the credit may be an advantage over contributing to an FSA account. When taxpayer's marginal tax rate is more than 15%, contributing to an FSA can be more advantageous, and in addition, contributions to an FSA reduce Social Security taxes at 7.65% provided taxpayer does not exceed the Social Security earnings maximum. This analysis should consider effects on earned income credit, refundable child

tax credit, and reduction of Social
Security tax.

Also, contributions to an FSA account
(1) must be used for dependent care
expenses or are forfeited and (2) the
FSA amount, once contributed, can
only be changed in very limited
circumstances.

## Nonrefundable Personal Credit Limit

Sec. 26(a) limits the amount of nonrefundable credits
in "this subpart" (Title 26, Chapter 1, Subchapter A,
Part IV, Subpart A, Nonrefundable Personal Credits)
to taxpayer's regular tax liability, (including excess
advance premium tax credit repayment) reduced by the
foreign tax credit plus the alternative minimum tax of
Sec. 55(a). Line 47 of Form 1040 for 2016 includes the
sum of the regular income tax, the alternative
minimum tax, and the excess advance premium tax
credit prior to allowing nonrefundable credits, the first
of which is foreign tax credit, with the second being
credit for child and dependent care. To the extent the
sum of the regular income tax, the alternative
minimum tax, and the excess advance premium tax
credit recapture, reduced by foreign tax credit, exceeds
the amount of the child and dependent care credit, the
full amount of such credit is allowed.

There is no carryback or carryover of child and
dependent care credit to the extent disallowed by this
limitation.

## Other Limitations and Applications

Married couples must file a joint return to claim the credit.[210] A married individual living apart may claim the credit on a separate return (1) provided such individual maintains (provides over half the maintenance costs) a household, (2) the household is the principal place of abode (for more than half a year) for a qualifying individual, and (3) the spouse is absent for the last six months of the year.[211] This requirement is very similar to the head of household filing requirements that allow a married taxpayer to qualify as not married. For the child and dependent care credit, the household must be maintained for a qualifying individual,[212] while the head of household requires the household be maintained for a child (within the meaning of Sec. 152(f)(1)).[213]

Divorced or legally separated parents can claim the credit for a child under age 13 or a child who is physically or mentally incapable of self-care. The child (1) must receive more than half of his or her support from parents, (2) be in the custody of one or both parents for more than half the calendar year resulting in him or her being a qualifying individual of the parent having the longer custody. The custodial parent can claim the credit even if the dependency exemption is released to the noncustodial parent.[214]

---

[210] IRC Sec. 21(e)(2).

[211] IRC Sec. 21(e)(4).

[212] Id.

[213] IRC Sec. 7703(b)(1).

[214] IRC Sec. 21(e)(5).

The care provider's name, address, and taxpayer identification number (not required if provider is a tax-exempt provider) must be provided on the claiming taxpayer's tax return. The taxpayer can provide what information is available and include a statement that the information was requested, but not provided.[215] In addition, the qualifying individual's taxpayer identification number must be provided.[216]

## Effect of Proposed Regulations

Proposed regulations remove existing wording in the regulations that refer to wording requiring that a taxpayer had to maintain a household for years beginning before January 1, 2005.

---

[215] IRC Sec. 21(e)(9).

[216] IRC Sec. 21(e)(10).

## Chapter 8

## Earned Income Tax Credit (EIC)

## Introduction

Congress enacted the earned income tax credit in 1975 as Code Sec. 32. It was enacted to eliminate some disincentives that may have encouraged low-income individuals to avoid employment. In addition, since the credit was refundable, it helped to offset social security taxes that low-income individuals had to pay when they paid little or no income tax when their income was offset by dependency exemptions and standard deductions. The credit has seen many adjustments since original enactment, with 1993 being a major adjustment.

## Eligibility Requirements for Taxpayers with and without Children

All taxpayers with and without children must meet certain requirements to file for the earned income tax credit. These requirements for eligible individuals are:

1) Must have earned income
2) Must have a valid social security number
3) Cannot file as married filing separately
4) Must be a U.S. citizen or resident alien for the entire year
5) Cannot claim foreign income exclusion by filing Form 2555 or Form 2555-EZ

6) Investment or "disqualified income", discussed later, cannot exceed $3,350 for 2014; $3,400 for 2015 and 2016; $3,450 for 2017.

7) Must have an abode in U.S. for more than half the tax year (U.S. Armed Forces are considered to have a U.S. abode when stationed outside the U.S. on extended active duty)

8) Must be age 25 and less than 65 before the end of the tax year. For a joint return, only one spouse needs to satisfy the age requirement

9) Cannot be someone who another taxpayer can claim as a dependency exemption,

10) Cannot be a nonresident alien.[217]

**Earned Income**

Taxpayers, single or married filing jointly, must have earned income with or without a qualifying child that is included in gross income to be eligible for the credit. Earned income for purposes of the earned income credit is:

1) Wages, salaries, tips, and other employee compensation if such amounts are included in gross income,

2) Net earnings from self-employment less the deduction for one-half the self-employment tax,

---

[217] IRS Pub 17 (2016), Chapter 36 and IRC Sec. 32(c).

3) Self-employment losses reduce earned income,[218]
4) Taxpayers may elect to treat nontaxable combat pay as earned income.[219]
5) Disability benefits received when employer's disability insurance plan pays policy premiums (benefits are taxable)[220]
6) Strike benefits paid to union members who picketed or did not picket labor site[221]

Earned income excludes:

1) Pension, annuity, social security, and VA benefits,
2) Amounts subject to 30% withholding tax on income not connected with a U.S. business of nonresident alien individuals,
3) Alimony and child support,[222]

---

[218] Reg. Sec. 1.32-2(c)(2).

[219] IRC Sec. 32(c)(2)(A) and Sec. 32(c)(2)(B)(vi). The combat pay remains exempt from federal taxes. All or none of the combat pay must be included for this purpose. Taxpayers cannot treat a portion of combat pay to maximize the earned income credit. IRS FS-2011-08, 2011 IRB Lexis 65, January 1, 2011.

[220] Chief Counsel Advice 199916041. Nontaxable disability benefits that result when employee pays part or all of disability insurance premiums are not considered earned income. (Same reference)

[221] Rev. Rul. 78-191, 1978-1 CB 8.

[222] IRS Pub 596 (2016), p 8.

4) Unemployment or workers' compensation benefits,[223]
5) Veterans' benefits,[224]
6) Amounts earned while an inmate is in a penal institution,
7) Housing and subsistence allowances for members of the armed forces,[225]
8) Jury duty fees,[226]
9) Rental income when taxpayer is not a real estate dealer or does not provide significant services to tenants,[227]
10) Welfare benefits,[228] and
11) Amounts received for "workfare" services to the extent subsidized by a state program.[229]

Earned income for earned income tax credit is determined without regard to any community property laws, meaning none of a spouse's earned income is included for this calculation if taxpayer resides in a community property state and does not file a joint return with a spouse.[230]

---

[223] Reg. Sec. 1.32-2(c)(2).

[224] IRS Pub. 596 (2016), p 8.

[225] IRS Pub 3 (2016), p 23.

[226] Service Center Advice 200028035.

[227] *Holbrook, Richard S.*, (2001), TC Summary Opinion, 2001-135.

[228] IRS Pub 596 (2016), p 8.

[229] IRC Sec. 32(c)(2)(B)(v) and IRS Pub 596 (2016), p 8.

[230] IRC Sec. 32(c)(2)(B)(i); Reg. Sec. 1.32-2(c)(2).

## Eligibility-Taxpayers without Children

Taxpayers without children qualify for a reduced amount of earned income credit. In addition to having earned income included in gross income, eligible individuals must:

1) Have a principal place of abode in the United States for more than one-half of the taxable year,
   a. There is no requirement that an eligible individual provide over half the cost of the abode.
   b. Members of the Armed Forces are deemed to have an abode in the U.S. during any period when stationed outside the U.S. while on active duty.
2) Not be a dependent on another taxpayer's tax return for the same year the credit is claimed. On a jointly filed return, neither taxpayer can be a dependent on another person's tax return even if the other person does not claim him or her as a dependent.[231]
3) Be at least 25 years of age and not more than 64 years old at the end of the taxable year. Only one eligible individual must meet the age requirement on a jointly filed return.[232]

---

[231] IRS Pub 596 (2016), Rule 13, p 16.

[232] IRC Sec. 32(c)(1)(A)(ii)(II).

## Eligibility-Taxpayers with Children

Taxpayers are allowed to claim the credit if they have a qualifying child or children. The child does not have to be a dependent of the claimant, but must:

1) Be a child, stepchild, a legally adopted child, foster child of the taxpayer, or a descendant of any such individual,
2) Satisfy the age requirements for a qualifying child in Sec. 152(c). The child must be (1) under age 19 at the close of the tax year, (2) less than 24 years old and a full-time student at the close of the taxable year, or (3) permanently and totally disabled during the tax year regardless of age, and (4) the qualifying child must be younger than the claiming eligible individual.
3) Share the same principal place of abode, located in the United States, with the taxpayer for more than one-half of the taxable year. This rule also applies for members of the Armed Forces.
4) Meet the joint return test of Sec. 152 (b)(2).[233]
5) Not be used by more than one person to claim the earned income credit.
6) Not be a qualifying child of another taxpayer. The tie-breaker rules of Sec. 152 (c)(4) are applied to determine which taxpayer can claim the qualifying child for the earned income

---

[233] IRS Pub 17, (2016), pgs 232, 234.

162

credit when two or more taxpayers can claim the same qualifying child.

7) Qualifying relatives do not qualify for the earned income credit.

Note the Sec. 152(c)(1)(D) requirement that the child cannot provide more than one-half of his or her own support does not apply for the earned income credit. In addition, the earned income credit is available to the custodial spouse if he or she allows the dependency exemption to the noncustodial spouse.

> **Example 8-1:** The earned income credit may be available to parent(s) in the year a college student graduates from college in May or June of a tax year. The student would probably provide more than 50% of his or her own support assuming they were employed after graduation, but this does not disqualify parents(s) from meeting this requirement, as the support test does not apply for the earned income credit. The child would have to satisfy the other earned income credit requirements discussed above. This allows an eligible individual to claim the earned income credit without an exemption deduction for a qualifying child.[234]

---

[234] IRC Sec. 32(c)(3)(A).

## Disqualified Income

Taxpayers with what is labeled "disqualified income" in excess of $3,350 for 2014, $3,400 for 2015 and 2016, and $3,450 for 2017 cannot claim the earned income credit.[235] Disqualified income includes:

1) Interest or dividends included in gross income for the taxable year,[236]
2) Interest received or accrued during the taxable year which is exempt from tax imposed by this chapter (Chapter 1 of the Internal Revenue Code),[237]
3) The excess, if any, of (i) gross income from rents or royalties not derived in the ordinary course of a trade or business, over (ii) the sum of noninterest deductions clearly and directly allocable to such gross income, plus properly allocable interest deductions to such gross income,[238]
4) Capital gain net income for the year (as defined in section 1222), but not gain treated as long-term capital gain for selling business assets,[239]
5) "The excess (if any) of (i) the aggregate income from all passive activities for the taxable year (

---

[235] IRC Sec. 32(i)(1).

[236] IRC Sec. 32(i)(2)(A).

[237] IRC Sec. 32(i)(2)(B).

[238] IRC Sec. 32(i)(2)(C).

[239] IRC Sec. 32(i)(2)(D) and Rev. Rul. 98-56, 1998-2, CB 667.

determined without regard to any amount included in earned income under subsection (c)(2), or described in a preceding subparagraph), over (ii) the aggregate losses from all passive activities for the taxable year (as so determined)."[240] (Author's comment—This is a direct quote of IRC Sec. 32(i)(2)(E). Subsection (c)(2) refers to Sec. 32(c)(2) while "preceding subparagraph" refers to subparagraphs within Sec. 32(i)(2).

## Other Requirements

Married individuals must file a joint return to claim the earned income credit.[241] This condition does not apply to an eligible individual who is considered unmarried under Sec. 7703(b) when certain married individuals live apart during the last six months of the year.[242] A taxpayer in this situation is treated the same as a single individual maintaining a household for a child. A taxpayer is considered unmarried for head of household purposes when married to a nonresident alien, but is considered married in such situation for earned income credit purposes. (See discussion of Diaz and Lozoya cases in Chapter 9)

---

[240] IRC Sec. 32(i)(2)(E).

[241] IRC Sec. 32(d).

[242] Reg. Sec. 1.32-2(b)(2).

A tax return must be a return for a full 12-month period to claim the credit, except for a short period return due to an individual's death.[243]

Taxpayers claiming the earned income credit must provide a taxpayer's (eligible individual's) identification number (TIN) or social security number, but not an individual taxpayer identification number (ITIN) or adoption taxpayer identification number (ATIN), and the age, name, and TIN (not ITIN or ATIN) for a qualifying child on the return.[244] Taxpayers claiming the credit must also attach Schedule EIC.

The earned income credit is not available for ten years after the credit was claimed fraudulently and two years for erroneously claimed credit due to intentional or reckless disregard of the rules.[245]

Paid tax return preparers must attach Form 8867, Paid Preparer's Earned Income Credit Checklist, with the federal return claiming earned income credit. Paid tax return preparers must maintain a copy of the due diligence check list. Tax preparers may be fined up to $510 (for 2016 and 2017) for failing to properly complete and retain Form 8867. In Mohamed, Tax Court Summary Opinion, 2017-69, Tax Court upheld

---

[243] IRC Sec. 32(e).

[244] IRC Secs. 32(m); 32(c)(1)(E);32(c)(1)(F);32(c)(3)(D).

[245] IRC Sec. 32(k).

due diligence penalty requirements of $7,000 for 14 returns.

The earned income credit is not available when married filing separately.

The earned income limitation amounts, phase-out amounts and the disqualified income amounts are adjusted for inflation.[246]

## Table Amounts and Comments

Tables of 2016 amounts related the earned income credit appear below.

## 2016 Taxpayers Not Filing as Married Filing Jointly

| Number of Qualifying Children | Income Range for Maximum Credit | Credit Rate | Maximum Credit | Phase-out Percent | Phase-out Range |
|---|---|---|---|---|---|
| None | $6,610-8,270 | 7.65% | $506 | 7.65% | $8,270-14,880 |
| 1 | $9,920-18,190 | 34.00 | $3,373 | 15.98 | $18,190-39,296 |
| 2 | $13,930-18,190 | 40.00 | $5,572 | 21.06 | $18,190-44,648 |
| 3 or more | $13,930-18,190 | 45.00 | $6,269 | 21.06 | $18,190-47,955 |

The "not filing as married filing jointly" includes filing as single, head of household, or qualifying widow(er)

---

[246] IRC Sec. 32(j).

as shown on an earned income credit table in the applicable instructions.

## 2016 Taxpayers Filing as Married Filing Jointly

| Number of Qualifying Children | Earned Income Range for Maximum Credit | Credit Rate | Maximum Credit | Phase-out Percent | Phase-out Range[247] |
|---|---|---|---|---|---|
| None | $6,610-13,820 | 7.65% | $506 | 7.65% | $13,820-20,430 |
| 1 | $9,920-23,740 | 34.00 | $3,373 | 15.98 | $23,740-44,846 |
| 2 | $13,930-23,740 | 40.00 | $5,572 | 21.06 | $23,740-50,198 |
| 3 or more | $13,930-23,740 | 45.00 | $6,269 | 21.06 | $23,740-53,505 |

Assume a married couple file jointly with two qualifying children. The earned income ranges for maximum credit of $13,930-23,740 result in the maximum credit of $5,572 throughout the entire range, obtained by taking 40% by $13,930. Once the greater of earned income or adjusted gross income exceeds $23,740, the credit reduces by 21.06% for each dollar of increase. The phase-out range is $26,458 wide, ($50,198-23,740), because 21.06% applied to $26,458 equals $5,572 the maximum amount of the credit. At $50,198 or more of earned income or adjusted gross

---

[247] The excess of the amount of the taxpayer's AGI (or earned income, if greater) over the phase-out range. In *Petty v. Comm.*, 87 T.C.M. 1419 (2004), taxpayer had to include gambling winnings in adjusted gross income increasing AGI to completely phase-out the earned income credit.

income (whichever is greater), the taxpayers lose all of their earned income credit.

The earned income credit amount is based solely on earned income while the reduction in the credit starts with the higher of AGI or earned income.[248]

> **Example 8-2:** Assume a married couple with two qualifying children has $39,000 of AGI. Their maximum earned income credit is $5,572. They are 57.7% ($39,000-23,740)/ ($26,458, as calculated above) into the phase-out range, resulting in a credit reduction of 57.7% of $5,572, or $3,215, resulting in $2,357 of earned income credit. If earned income had been higher than $39,000, the reduction would be 21.06% of the higher amount. The actual earned income credit amount is determined using tables.[249]

Tables of 2017 amounts related the earned income credit appear below.

---

[248] IRC Sec. 32(a)(2).

[249] IRC Sec. 32(f).

## 2017 Taxpayers Not Filing as Married Filing Jointly

| Number of Qualifying Children | Income Range for Maximum Credit | Credit Rate | Maximum Credit | Phase-out Percent | Phase-out Range |
|---|---|---|---|---|---|
| None | $6,670-8,340 | 7.65% | $510 | 7.65% | $8,340-15,010 |
| 1 | $10,000-18,340 | 34.00 | $3,400 | 15.98 | $18,340-39,617 |
| 2 | $14,040-18,340 | 40.00 | $5,616 | 21.06 | $18,340-45,007 |
| 3 or more | $14,040-18,340 | 45.00 | $6,318 | 21.06 | $18,340-48,340 |

## 2017 Taxpayers Filing as Married Filing Jointly

| Number of Qualifying Children | Earned Income Range for Maximum Credit | Credit Rate | Maximum Credit | Phase-out Percent | Phase-out Range |
|---|---|---|---|---|---|
| None | $6,670-13,930 | 7.65% | $510 | 7.65% | $13,930-20,600 |
| 1 | $10,000-23,930 | 34.00 | $3,400 | 15.98 | $23,930-45,207 |
| 2 | $14,040-23,930 | 40.00 | $5,616 | 21.06 | $23,930-50,597 |
| 3 or more | $14,040-23,930 | 45.00 | $6,318 | 21.06 | $23,930-53,930 |

The calculations shown above for the 2016 tables would be the same for the 2017 tables, except 2017 table amounts would be used instead of 2016 amounts.

## Optional Method for Social Security Coverage

The IRS allows taxpayers two optional methods for Social Security coverage when taxpayers have a loss or a small amount self-employment income. The use of these methods also allows taxpayers to qualify to claim the earned income credit or may provide a larger credit. In addition, the use of the optional method may result in higher additional child tax credit and child and dependent care credit. (IRS Pub 334 (2016), p 42). The use of the optional method for Social Security coverage will result in paying self-employment tax. Taxpayers must calculate these credits with and without the optional method to determine the maximum credit amounts. (See instructions for Form 1040, Schedule SE)

### Effect of Proposed Regulations

The proposed regulations conform the Sec. 32 regulations to WFTRA amendments to Sec. 32. In addition, paragraphs relating to advance payment of the earned income credit are removed as this requirement was repealed by Sec. 3507 of the FAA Air Transportation Modernization and Safety Improvement Act.

If an individual meets the qualifying child for more than one taxpayer, tiebreaker rules in Sec. 152 (moved from Sec. 32 to Sec. 152(c)(4) by WFTRA) determined which taxpayer was allowed to claim the individual as a qualifying child for EIC. In this situation, with no regulatory guidance, the IRS, since 1995, took the position that the person not allowed to claim a qualifying child for the EIC under the tiebreaker rules was precluded from claiming the childless EIC. (IRS Proposed regulations REG-137604-07). The proposed regulations remove this IRS treatment, allowing the

171

individual to claim childless EIC. Examples are included in the proposed regulations discussing this application.

## 2017 Disaster Tax Relief

The Disaster Tax Relief and Airport and Airway Extension Act of 2017 (P.L. 115-63) was signed by President Trump on September 29, 2017. The Act provides special tax relief to taxpayers who resided in hurricane areas in 2017.

Qualified individuals are defined as taxpayers whose principal place of abode on Aug 23, 2017 was located in the Hurricane Harvey disaster zone, or in the Hurricane Harvey disaster area and were displaced from their principal place of abode by Hurricane Harvey. This provision also applies to Hurricane Irma individuals using a Sept. 5, 2017 date and Hurricane Maria individuals using a Sept. 16, 2017 date.

Taxpayers must have earned income to claim the earned income credit (Sec. 32) and earned income to claim refundable child tax credit (Sec. 24). If the taxpayers' earned income for the year which includes the applicable dates shown is less than earned income for the preceding tax year, the taxpayer can substitute the earned income for the preceding tax year for earned income for the tax year that includes the applicable date shown above. If this provision is elected, it applies for both the earned income credit treatment and refundable child tax credit. Only one person on a joint return has to be qualified individual.

## Chapter 9

## Head of Household Filing Status

The head of household filing status must be considered whenever a taxpayer is unmarried (or considered unmarried) and maintains a household which is the principal place of abode for a qualifying person. A qualifying person includes a claimant's child and a parent that can be claimed for a dependency exemption.

The head of household filing status is available when a taxpayer is (1) unmarried (or treated as unmarried) at the end of the tax year; (2) not a surviving spouse; (3) not a nonresident alien at any time during such tax year; and (4) maintains a household for a qualifying person.

### Unmarried (or Considered Unmarried)

An individual is considered unmarried if all of the conditions are satisfied:

a) He or she files a separate return that is, filing as married filing separately, single, or head of household
b) He or she paid more than half the cost of keeping up a home for the tax year
c) A spouse, if still married, did not live in the home during the last six months of the tax year

d) The home was the main home of a child or
other qualifying dependent including stepchild,
foster child, and a parent for more than half the
year. A parent can live in a separate facility
provided the taxpayer can claim the parent as a
dependent

e) He or she must be able to claim a dependency
exemption for the child or other qualifying
dependent, except a custodial parent who
allows the noncustodial parent to claim the
dependency exemption for a child, still
qualifies for head of household filing status if
all other conditions are satisfied.[250]

A special rule applies when one spouse is a nonresident
alien anytime during the year and no election is made
to treat the nonresident spouse as a resident alien. The
other spouse is considered unmarried for head of
household purposes. However, the nonresident alien
spouse is not a qualifying person for the head of
household filing status, so the claiming taxpayer must
have another qualifying person and meet the other tests
to be eligible to file as a head of household.[251]

> **Example 9-1:** Assume a U.S citizen,
> Justin, is married to a nonresident alien
> spouse, Diana. They have two children
> who are U.S. citizens. They reside in
> China. Justin is considered unmarried,

---

[250] IRS Pub 17 (2016), p 23.

[251] Id. p 23 and IRC Sec. 2 (b)(2)(B).

for head of household filing purposes, as Diana is a nonresident alien. Assuming all head of household tests are satisfied, Justin can file using head of household filing status. Moreover, he can claim a dependency exemption for Diana provided Diana has no gross income for U.S. tax purposes, is not filing a return, and is not a dependent of another taxpayer.[252]

**Observation:** A person married to a nonresident alien, as described in the above example, is considered unmarried for head of household purposes. However, for purposes of the earned income credit Justin is considered married. Married taxpayers must file a joint return to claim the earned income credit.[253]

**Observation:** A taxpayer who elects to treat a nonresident alien spouse as a resident alien can file a joint tax return for the tax year. See IRS Pub 54 (2016), pgs. 6-7

Two tax court cases compare situations related to head of household filing status and the earned income credit.

---

[252] IRS Pub 501 (2016), p 11.

[253] Id. Pub 17 (2016), p 232.

In *Elpidio Lozoya v. Commissioner*, Lozoya's spouse was an illegal alien and, based on the evidence, did not reside in residence for the last six months of the year. Lozoya satisfied the head of household rules, including the six-month rule of Sec. 7703(b), and filed his return as head of household claiming the earned income credit.

In *Manuel Diaz*, Diaz was married to a nonresident alien, and qualified for head of household filing status, but could not claim the earned income credit, as they did not live apart for the last six months of the year.[254]

**Not Be a Surviving Spouse**

An individual cannot be a surviving spouse and qualify for head of household filing status.[255] A surviving spouse can file as married filing jointly in the year the spouse dies.[256] If the surviving spouse has dependent children, he or she may be able to file as qualifying widow(er) for two years after the year in which the spouse dies and is able to use rates applicable to married filing jointly.

---

[254] *Elpidio Lozoya v. Comm.*, T.C. Summary Opinion 2005-73 and *Manuel Diaz*, TCM 2004-145. Also see, James M. Hopkins, *Head of Household Legally Married, but not [sic]*, Spring 2005, pgs. 34-37., *NATP TAXPRO Journal*, National Association of Tax Professionals.

[255] Sec. 2(b)(1).

[256] IRS Pub 501 (2016), p 10.

## Not Be a Nonresident Alien

Head of household filing status is not available to any taxpayer who is a nonresident alien at any time during the year.[257]

## Maintain a Household for the Taxpayer and Qualifying Person

In regard to the household:
a) the taxpayer must pay over half the cost of maintaining a household for the year
b) (1) the taxpayer's qualifying child or (2) an individual (qualifying person) for whom the taxpayer can claim a dependency exemption must live in the household for over half the year[258] or
c) may be a separate household for a father or mother if the taxpayer can claim a dependency exemption for that parent.[259]

The costs of maintaining a household include:
- Real estate taxes
- Mortgage interest
- Rent
- Utilities
- Repairs and maintenance
- Household property insurance

---

[257] IRC Sec. 2(b)(3)(A).

[258] IRC Sec. 2(b)(1)(A).

[259] IRC Sec. 2(b)(1)(B).

- Food consumed on the premises
- Other expense related to maintaining the household

Public assistance program payments for maintaining the household cannot be counted as provided by the taxpayer, but must be counted in the total cost of maintaining the household to see if the taxpayer provided over half the cost.

Can a single residence location result in multiple head of household qualifications? The answer is affirmative with proper planning. In *Estate of Flemming,*[260] two families, the Flemmings and the Merckes, lived in the same residential location. The Flemmings consisted of a mother (who passed away before the filing of the Tax Court case) and her unmarried daughter. The Merckes consisted of the deceased woman's married daughter, her husband, and their three children. The two parties contributed equally to the maintenance of the property. The Flemmings paid one-third and the Merckes paid two-thirds of the food, utilities, and servant pay. The Tax Court interpreted "household" in a favorable, reasonable manner, as the term lacked a precise meaning.

> **Observation:** Important issues to consider in planning for more than one

---

[260] In *Estate of Flemming, v. Comm,* (1974), 33 TCM 619, Acq. Also see Service Center Advice (SCA) 1998-041. Proposed Regulation Sec. 1.2-2(d)(5)(i) and (ii) discuss separate head of households from one shared residence.

head of household filing status for one
physical residence include:

- The residence must be a home for each
family and be a principal place of abode
for one or more of each family's
children or other qualifying individual.
- Each family must act independently in
non-household related matters, such as
separate phone lines, Christmas cards,
magazine subscriptions, and the like.
- There must be common areas for all
household members and separate adult
areas.
- Each party must keep detailed records
to show each separate party had a
separate part of the household and how
costs were shared between separate
households.[261]

The Flemming case was decided in 1974 when a head
of household claimant did not have to have a
dependency exemption for a qualifying individual to
claim head of household filing status.

A key to having two heads of household within a single
residence is the two taxpayers must have separate
families. An unmarried boyfriend and girlfriend with
separate families from prior relationships living

---

[261] Id.

together in the same household would probably not satisfy the above requirements.

When two unmarried families, A and B live together in a shared dwelling each with respective dependent families, A must prove A contributed over one-half of the household expenses jointly contributed by A and A's children. B and B's children must prove B and B's children contributed over one-half the household expenses contributed jointly by B and B's children. Neither A or B are required to prove they contributed over one-half of the total costs of maintaining the shared dwelling.[262]

## Qualifying Person for Head of Household Purposes

A qualifying person can be a (1) unmarried child, (2) married child, or (3) other related dependent, or (4) a parent.

An unmarried child must meet the dependency exemption requirements of Sec. 152 (c), without the application of Sec. 152(e), (1) relationship; (2) same principal place of abode as the taxpayer for more than half the tax year; (3) age test; and (4) must not have provided more than half of his or her own support. The unmarried child meeting these tests is known as a

---

[262] Service Center Advice 1998-041.

qualifying child for dependency purposes and a qualifying person for head of household purposes.[263]

> **Observation:** A qualifying child is defined in IRC Sec. 152 (c) without regard to IRC Sec. 152 (e). Sec. 152 (e) pertains to a dependency exemption for divorced, separated, or never married parents. If the qualifying child's custodial parent completes Form 8332 and all other necessary requirements are satisfied allowing the noncustodial parent to a dependency exemption for the qualifying child, the ability to use the head of household filing status stays with the custodial parent.[264]

> **Observation:** Head of household filing status is not available if the qualifying person (1) is married at the end of the taxpayer's tax year and cannot be claimed as a dependent because he or she filed a joint return with a spouse or (2) is not a U.S. citizen or resident.[265] A taxpayer with a married child who could be a qualifying person for head of

---

[263] IRC Sec. 2(b).

[264] See IRS Notice 2006-86, 2006-2 C.B. 680. (Notice 2006-86 will be obsolete by the proposed regulations.) See Proposed Regulations 1.152-2(g)(3) and (4).

[265] IRC Sec. 2(b)(1)(A)(i)(I)(II).

household filing status should compare the benefits of having the qualifying person not file a joint return with his or her spouse, but file as married filing separately, thus allowing the taxpayer to file as head of household, if that filing alternative yields larger tax savings.

**Observation:** Sec. 152(c)(1)(E) provides a married qualifying child can be a qualifying child dependent if he or she has not filed a joint return (other than only a claim of refund) with the individual's spouse under section 6013 for the taxable year beginning in the calendar year in which the taxable year of the taxpayer begins. Sec. 2(b)(1)(A)(i)(I)(II) denies head of household status to a potential claiming individual if his or her qualifying person is married at the close of the taxpayer's taxable year and is not a dependent by reason of section of 152(b)(2), joint return with spouse, or (b)(3), not a citizen or national of the United States, or both. Sec. 2(b) where head of household status is defined provides no mention for allowing a married, qualifying child filing a joint return with his or her spouse that is a claim for refund to be a qualifying person for head of household filing

status. However, IRS 2016 Pub. 17,
page 24, indicates a married qualifying
child is a qualifying person for head of
household purposes if the claiming
taxpayer can claim an exemption for the
married child.

The other related dependent category consists of
qualifying relative relationships listed in Sec. 152(d),
other than Sec. 152 (d)(2)(H), unrelated member of
taxpayer's household. This includes taxpayer's
brother, sister, stepbrother, stepsister, father or mother,
including ancestors of either, stepfather, stepmother,
sons and daughters of taxpayer's brother or sisters,
brother or sister of taxpayer's father or mother,
taxpayer's in-laws: son, daughter, mother, father, sister
or brother. Sec 2(b)(3), defining head of household,
prevents head of household filing status for an
unrelated dependent who qualifies for a dependency
exemption as a result of living with a taxpayer for the
entire taxable year and in multiple support situations.[266]

> **Observation:** An unmarried taxpayer
> was allowed head of household filing
> status for a niece who lived with him for
> at least six months of the tax year.[267] A
> taxpayer was allowed an exemption for
> a cousin (lived with taxpayer the entire

---

[266] IRC Sec. 2(b)(3)(B)(i)(ii).

[267] *Hubbard, Marvin B.*, TC Summary Opinion 2004-148
(2004).

tax year), but not allowed head of household filing status.[268]

Taxpayer's parent can be a qualifying person provided the taxpayer maintains a household (that can be within taxpayer's abode) or a separate household (apartment or care facility) that is the principal place of abode for a parent provided the taxpayer is entitled to a dependency exemption for the parent. In this situation, the parent does not have to reside with the taxpayer.

## Amending HOH filed Tax Return to Married Filing Jointly

Taxpayer in *Ibrahim v. Commissioner*, T.C. Memo 2014-8, reversed, CA-8, June 10, 2015, allowed taxpayer to amend a mistaken filing as head-of-household to a married filing joint return to claim a credit and refund. The Tax Court treated the head-of-household return as a separate return, denying taxpayer the ability to amend and change filing status to married filing jointly. Sec. 6013(b) prohibits joint returns after taxpayer has filed a "separate return". The 8th Circuit did a thorough analysis and determined a "separate return" was limited to a "married filing separately" return. As the taxpayer never filed as married filing separately, he was allowed to amend his head-of-household and file as married filing jointly. The 8th Circuit stated ..." that "separate return" refers only to married filing separately. See section 1(d),

---

[268] *Keegan, Karen Ann*, TCM 1997-511(1997).

6654(d)(1)(C)(ii), 7703(b)". One-8th Circuit judge dissented with final decision, concluding it was reasonable to interpret any non-joint return, including head-of household returns, as separate returns.

In *Knez*, T.C. Memo 2017-205, the Tax Court ruled Knez, a married taxpayer, who filed as head of household, had not filed a separate return for purposes of Sec. 6013(b) and was allowed to file a joint return for that tax year.

## Qualifying Person for Years beginning prior to January 1, 2005

A taxpayer maintaining his or her own household that was also a principal place of abode for a son, stepson, daughter, stepdaughter of the taxpayer, or their descendants qualified taxpayer for head of household filing status regardless of whether taxpayer could claim them for a dependency exemption. [269] Modified rules applied if the household residents, as listed above, were married.

## Effect of Proposed Regulations

The proposed regulations amend Sec. 2 regulations to update the definitions of surviving spouse and head of household to conform to WFTRA amendments. References in the regulations in Secs. 2, 3, and 6013 remove references that the return of a surviving spouse should be treated as a joint return.

---

[269] Baker, Joel, TCM 1997-3, (1997) law in effect prior to January 1, 2005.

The regulations referring to maintaining a household are revised and moved from Sec. 21 to Sec. 2 regulations. This removes these regulations from Sec. 21, as WFTRA removed the requirement that a taxpayer maintain a household to claim Sec. 21 credit (child and dependent care to be gainfully employed).

The proposed regulations also discuss who is a qualifying child or dependent, a parent, marital status, nonresident alien spouse, member of the household, and issues where an individual is a member of the household for less than a full year.

The proposed regulations also discuss how to determine more than one-half of the costs related to operating the household, including when a dependent resides in the house for less than a full year.

The proposed regulations contain a new section discussing a shared residence (with examples) that would allow certain taxpayers not filing a joint return to qualify for head of household status when sharing a residence. Prop. Reg. 1.2-2(d)(5)(i) and (ii).

# Appendix 1

## Eligibility Table for Child Tax Law Benefits

| Test | Exemption | (EITC) | Child Tax Credit | Child Care Credit | Dependent Care Benefits Income Exclusion | HH Status |
|---|---|---|---|---|---|---|
| Age Test | Under 19 or under 24 if a full-time student for at least five months, and younger than claiming taxpayer (or your spouse, if filing jointly). Age test does not apply if child is permanently and totally disabled. | Under 19 or under 24 if a full-time student for at least five months, and younger than claiming taxpayer (or your spouse, if filing jointly). Age test does not apply if child is permanently and totally disabled. | Child must be under age 17 at the end of the tax year and child must be younger than claiming taxpayer (or your spouse, if filing jointly). | 1. Taxpayer's qualifying child dependent must be under age 13 when the care is provided. 2. Taxpayer's dependent who is physically and mentally incapable of self-care and has same place of abode as the taxpayer for more than half year regardless of age. (SEE Below) 3. Taxpayer's spouse who is physically and mentally incapable of self-care and has same place of abode as the taxpayer for more than half year regardless of age | 1. Taxpayer's qualifying child dependent must be under age 13 when the care is provided. 2. Taxpayer's spouse who is physically and mentally incapable of self-care and has same place of abode as the taxpayer for more than half year regardless of age 3. Taxpayer's dependent who is physically and mentally incapable of self-care and has same place of abode as the taxpayer for more than half year regardless of age. (SEE Below) | Must meet age tests for qualifying child Age test does not apply to qualifying relative. Any age if permanently and totally disabled. |
| Relationship | Must be taxpayer's child, stepchild, foster child, sibling, stepsibling, or descendant of any of them. Adopted children are treated as taxpayer's own children. This is for a | Must be taxpayer's child, stepchild, foster child, sibling, stepsibling, or descendant of any of them. Adopted children are treated as | Must be taxpayer's child, stepchild, foster child, sibling, stepsibling, or descendant of any of them. Adopted children are treated as | Must be taxpayer's child, stepchild, foster child, sibling, stepsibling, or descendant of any of them. Spouse, as described above, also qualifies | Must be taxpayer's child, stepchild, foster child, sibling, stepsibling, or descendant of any of them. Spouse, as described above, also qualifies | Broader rules for qualifying relatives apply. Note: HOH is not available to dependent not related to taxpayer who qualifies as a dependent by being a |

| Test | Exemption | (EITC) | Child Tax Credit | Child Care Credit | Dependent Care Benefits Income Exclusion | HH Status |
|---|---|---|---|---|---|---|
| | qualifying child. Qualifying relative definition is broader. | taxpayer's own child. | taxpayer's own child. | | | member of taxpayer's household for entire taxable year. Also exemption allowed by a multiple support agreement does not qualify taxpayer for HOH status. |
| Residence test | Child must live with taxpayer for at least six months during the year. Temporary absences count as time lived with the taxpayer. Different rule applies to children of divorced, separated, or never married parents. | Child must live with taxpayer for at least six months during the year. Temporary absences count as time lived with the taxpayer. Abode must be in the USA (50 states and the District of Columbia). | Child must live with taxpayer for at least six months during the year. Temporary absences count as time lived the taxpayer. Different rule applies to children of divorced, separated, or never married parents. | Child or spouse must live with taxpayer for at least six months during the year. See below for divorced parents. | Child or spouse must live with taxpayer for at least six months during the year. | Qualifying person for HOH must live with taxpayer for more than one-half the taxable. See exception below for parent of taxpayer. |
| Support test | Child cannot be self-supporting, that is, must provide less than half of own support. | Support test does not apply. | Child cannot be self-supporting, that is, must provide less than half of own support. | Child cannot be self-supporting, that is, child must provide less than half of own support. | Child cannot be self-supporting, that is, must provide less than half of own support. | QC cannot provide more than one-half support. Taxpayer must provide over one-half support for a QR dependent. |
| Citizen or resident test | Dependent must be U.S. citizen/national/resident or a resident of Mexico or Canada. | No. Child must have Social Security number. | Dependent must be U.S. citizen/national/resident alien. Cannot be resident of Mexico, Canada or | Dependent must be U.S. citizen/national/resident or a resident of Mexico or Canada. | Dependent must be U.S. citizen/national/resident or a resident of Mexico or Canada. | QC and QR must be a U.S. citizen or resident of U.S. or countries contiguous to the U.S. |

188

| Test | Exemption | (EITC) | Child Tax Credit | Child Care Credit | Dependent Care Benefits Income Exclusion | HH Status |
|---|---|---|---|---|---|---|
| | | | any other country. Note this difference for child tax credit and for dependency exemption. | | | |
| Taxpayer income limitation | 2017 exemption amounts are reduced as AGI exceeds $156,900 for MFS; $261,500 for Single; $287,650 for HOH; $313,800 for MFJ. No exemption amounts allowed for alternative minimum tax. | Credit is phased out based on higher of AGI or earned income amount, filing status and number of qualifying children. | Credit reduced by $50 for each $1,000, or fraction thereof, of MAGI over $110,000 for MFJ; $75,000 for single/head of household/qu alifying widow(er); $55,000 for married filing separately. | Credit percentage is 35% of work-related expenses if AGI is < or equal to $15,000. Percentage declines by 1% for each $2,000 of additional AGI. For AGI above $43,000, percentage is capped at 20%. | None | No limitation or reduction on HOH benefits based taxpayer's AGI. |
| Dependent's gross income | No limitation for qualifying child; Cannot exceed exemption amount for qualifying relative. | No limitation for qualifying child. Qualifying relative dependents do not qualify for this benefit. | No income limitation for qualifying child. Qualifying relative dependents do not qualify for this benefit. | No limitation. | No limitation | QR dependent's income cannot exceed annual exemption amount. No limit on QC's gross income, provided QC does not provide more than one-half of support. |
| Other requirements | None | 1. Eligible individual taxpayer (EI). Must have earned income. 2. EI must have valid SSN. 3. EI must be a U.S. citizen or resident alien. 4. No credit if investment | None | 1. Work related expenses capped: $3,000 for one qualifying person; $6,000 for two or more qualifying persons. 2. Work related expenses cannot exceed | 1 Must have earned income. 2. Taxpayer can exclude $5,000 ($2,500 for MFS returns) from gross income for child and dependent care services under an employer plan and paid by an | 1. Taxpayer is not married or a surviving spouse at year end. 2. Taxpayer must maintain a household for more than one-half of taxable year that is the principal place of abode for a |

189

| Test | Exemption | (EITC) | Child Tax Credit | Child Care Credit | Dependent Care Benefits Income Exclusion | HH Status |
|---|---|---|---|---|---|---|
| | | income exceeds $3,350 for 2014; $3,400 for 2015 & 2016; $3,450 for 2017 5. No credit for taxpayers who claim foreign income exclusion. 6. If married, must file joint return. 7.If one spouse is a nonresident alien, must file a joint return to claim credit 8. Not available to married filing separately. 9. Lower credit available with no qualifying children. 10. Tax return must cover full 12-month period, unless short-period is caused by taxpayer's death. | | earned income of lower earned income on return. Special earned income rules apply to (a) full-time student spouse and (2) a nonworking physically and mentally incapable of self-care spouse. 3. Married taxpayer must file a joint return to claim the credit. 4. Work related expenses must be reduced by total of dependent care assistance benefits excluded from gross income. 5.Taxpayer must have earned income. | employer. Exclusion amount limited to $3,000 if only one qualifying person. 3. Exclusion cannot exceed employee's earned income (earned income of the lower earning spouse on a joint return). | qualifying person. 3. Qualifying person(QP) is a qualifying child (QC), defined in Sec. 152(c) without regard to Sec. 152(e) relating to specialized rules for divorced taxpayers; QC cannot be married at the close of the taxable year and file joint return with spouse, except for refund of tax and no tax liability. 4. Taxpayer who supports parent in a separate location and who can claim him or her as a dependent can qualify for HOH. This is an exception to living with the HOH claiming taxpayer for more than one-half the taxable year. 5. Claiming taxpayer cannot be a nonresident alien. 6. Taxpayer is considered not married if spouse is a nonresident alien at any time during |

| Test | Exemption | (EITC) | Child Tax Credit | Child Care Credit | Dependent Care Benefits Income Exclusion | HH Status |
|------|-----------|--------|------------------|-------------------|-------------------------------------------|-----------|
|      |           |        |                  |                   |                                           | the taxable year, but must have qualifying child/relative dependent. |

**Comments to Table Entries**

**Earned Income Credit:**

1. Earned income credit is a refundable credit.

2. The support test does not apply; only the relationship, residency test, as modified, and age tests of the dependency exemption tests apply.

3. The residency test is limited to the 50 states and District of Columbia. Residences outside the United States are not eligible for the credit.

4. Taxpayer can claim an exemption for a married child (unless Form 8332 was completed giving the exemption to the noncustodial parent) even if married child files a joint return to claim a refund of withheld income tax and no tax liability is shown on a separate return. Form 8332 releases the exemption and child tax credit to the noncustodial parent. All other child tax benefits (head of household filing status, if applicable), child and dependent care credit and exclusion of employer benefits, and earned income tax credit stay with the custodial parent.[270]

---

[270] IRS Pub. 17 (2016), pgs. 28, 32; IRS Notice 2006-86, p 680. Notice 2006-86 does not mention education credits. (Notice 2006-86 will be obsolete by the proposed

## Child Tax Credit

1. The qualifying child must be claimed on the taxpayer's return. When Form 8332 is completed, shifting the exemption to the noncustodial parent, the noncustodial parent is also eligible to claim the child tax credit because of this rule.

2. Married qualifying child can file joint return with spouse to claim a refund of withheld income tax and no tax liability is shown on the return or on a MFS return.

3. For divorced, separated, or parents who were never married, the custodial parent has custody of the child. The custodial parent can complete Form 8332 giving the dependency exemption and child tax credit to the noncustodial parent.

---

regulations.) A person who can be claimed for a dependency exemption by another taxpayer cannot claim education credits. IRC Sec. 25A(g)(3). Educational expenses paid the dependent are considered paid by the taxpayer claiming the dependency exemption. A custodial parent signing Form 8332 releasing the dependency exemption to the noncustodial parent would allow the noncustodial parent to claim any educational credits provided other credit requirements are satisfied. Any qualified education expenses paid directly to the educational institution by a former spouse not claiming a dependency exemption for the student are deemed paid by the student and would be counted by the noncustodial parent for education credits. Reg. Sec. 1.25A-5(b)

## Child and Dependent Care Credit

1. A third category of qualifying person is (a) a person physically or mentally unable to perform self-care for himself or herself who lived with the taxpayer for more than half the year and is taxpayer's dependent. The Sec. 152 dependency tests of (1) claimed dependent cannot claim any dependents, (2) dependent is married and files a joint return with spouse, and (3) the gross income test for a qualifying relative are not considered.[271]

2. For parents who are divorced, separated, or never married, this credit is available to the custodial parent, assuming all tests are satisfied. If the custodial parent files a Form 8332 given the dependency exemption to the noncustodial spouse, this credit stays with the custodial parent.

3. The amount of the child and dependent credit offsets the taxpayer's regular income tax, plus the alternative minimum tax and excess advance premium tax credit repayment, less the foreign tax credit. Any child and dependent care credit in excess of the above limitation is

---

[271] IRC Sec 21(b)(1)(B)

lost. (See 2016 instructions for Form 2441, page 4)

4. IRC Sec. 26(a). For tax years beginning after December 31, 2011, all nonrefundable personal tax credits are allowed to the full extent of the taxpayer's regular income tax liability (including excess advance premium credit repayments), reduced by the foreign tax credit, plus the alternative minimum tax. Special calculations are necessary to determine the amount of the nonrefundable child tax credit when other nonrefundable credits are present. The starting point is the regular income tax plus the alternative minimum tax plus excess advance premium tax credit repayments. Line 47 on a 2016 Form 1040 includes the regular income tax, alternative minimum tax, and excess advance premium tax credit repayment. The sum of the following credits are subtracted from the Line 47 (2016 Form 1040) total in the following order: (1) foreign tax credit; (2) child and dependent care credit; (3) education credits; (4) retirement savings credit; (5) nonbusiness energy property credit (Form 5695, Part II, Line 30); (6) personal use alternative motor vehicle credit (Form 8910, Part III, Line 15; (7) personal use of qualified plug-in electric drive motor vehicle credit, Form 8936, Part III, Line 23; and (8) credit for the elderly and disabled, Schedule R, Line 22.

5. In addition, credits claimed for (a) mortgage interest credit, Form 8396; (b) adoption credit, Form 8839; (c) residential energy efficient property credit (Form 5695, Part I); and (d) District of Columbia first-time homebuyer credit, Form 8859; are also subtracted from the Form 1040 Line 47 total. The sum of these credits, in both these categories, reduces the Form 1040 Line 47 total to the amount of nonrefundable child credit that can be claimed. If any of these credits are present, a lower amount of nonrefundable child tax credit can be claimed on 2016 Form 1040 Line 52, increasing the potential amount of refundable child tax credit that can be claimed. (See 2016 Form 1040 Instructions, Form 1040 Child Tax Credit Worksheets, noting when the Child Tax Credit Worksheet in IRS Pub 972 (2016), pgs., 5-10, must be used instead of the worksheet in the Form 1040 instructions in certain circumstances.)

6. Applicable Internal Revenue Code Sections 2, 21, 24, 32, 151, and 152 appear on the following pages.

## Applicable IRC Sections

These Internal Revenue Code Sections are located at http://uscode.house.gov/   All amendment summaries are also located there. The sections are current as of November 2017.

### Sec.2 Definitions and special rules

### (a) Definition of surviving spouse

**(1) In general**--For purposes of section 1, the term "surviving spouse" means a taxpayer-

> (A) whose spouse died during either of his two taxable years immediately preceding the taxable year, and

> (B) who maintains as his home a household which constitutes for the taxable year the principal place of abode (as a member of such household) of a dependent (i) who (within the meaning of section 152, determined without regard to subsections (b)(1), (b)(2), and (d)(1)(B) thereof) is a son, stepson, daughter, or stepdaughter of the taxpayer, and (ii) with respect to whom the taxpayer is entitled to a deduction for the taxable year under section 151.

For purposes of this paragraph, an individual shall be considered as maintaining a household only if over half of the cost of maintaining the household during the taxable year is furnished by such individual.

**(2) Limitations**--Notwithstanding paragraph (1), for purposes of section 1 a taxpayer shall not be considered to be a surviving spouse-

(A) if the taxpayer has remarried at any time before the close of the taxable year, or

(B) unless, for the taxpayer's taxable year during which his spouse died, a joint return could have been made under the provisions of section 6013 (without regard to subsection (a)(3) thereof).

**(3) Special rule where deceased spouse was in missing status**

If an individual was in a missing status (within the meaning of section 6013(f)(3)) as a result of service in a combat zone (as determined for purposes of section 112) and if such individual remains in such status until the date referred to in subparagraph (A) or (B), then, for purposes of paragraph (1)(A), the date on which such individual died shall be treated as the earlier of the date determined under subparagraph (A) or the date determined under subparagraph (B):

(A) the date on which the determination is made under section 556 of title 37 of the United States Code or under section 5566 of title 5 of such Code (whichever is applicable) that such individual died while in such missing status, or

(B) except in the case of the combat zone designated for purposes of the Vietnam conflict, the date which is 2 years after the date designated under section 112 as the date of termination of combatant activities in that zone.

## (b) Definition of head of household

### (1) In general

For purposes of this subtitle, an individual shall be considered a head of a household if, and only if, such individual is not married at the close of his taxable year, is not a surviving spouse (as defined in subsection (a)), and either-

(A) maintains as his home a household which constitutes for more than one-half of such taxable year the principal place of abode, as a member of such household, of-

(i) a qualifying child of the individual (as defined in section 152(c), determined without regard to section 152(e)), but not if such child-

(I) is married at the close of the taxpayer's taxable year, and

(II) is not a dependent of such individual by reason of section 152(b)(2) or 152(b)(3), or both, or

(ii) any other person who is a dependent of the taxpayer, if the taxpayer is entitled to a deduction for the taxable year for such person under section 151, or

(B) maintains a household which constitutes for such taxable year the principal place of abode of the father or mother of the taxpayer, if the taxpayer is entitled to a deduction for the taxable year for such father or mother under section 151.

For purposes of this paragraph, an individual shall be considered as maintaining a household only if over half of the cost of maintaining the household during the taxable year is furnished by such individual.

**(2) Determination of status**

For purposes of this subsection-

(A) an individual who is legally separated from his spouse under a decree of divorce or of separate maintenance shall not be considered as married;

(B) a taxpayer shall be considered as not married at the close of his taxable year if at any time during the taxable year his spouse is a nonresident alien; and

(C) a taxpayer shall be considered as married at the close of his taxable year if his spouse (other than a spouse described in subparagraph (B)) died during the taxable year.

**(3) Limitations**

Notwithstanding paragraph (1), for purposes of this subtitle a taxpayer shall not be considered to be a head of a household-

(A) if at any time during the taxable year he is a nonresident alien; or

(B) by reason of an individual who would not be a dependent for the taxable year but for-

(i) subparagraph (H) of section 152(d)(2), or

(ii) paragraph (3) of section 152(d).

## (c) Certain married individuals living apart

For purposes of this part, an individual shall be treated as not married at the close of the taxable year if such individual is so treated under the provisions of section 7703(b).

## (d) Nonresident aliens

In the case of a nonresident alien individual, the taxes imposed by sections 1 and 55 shall apply only as provided by section 871 or 877.

## (e) Cross reference

**For definition of taxable income, see section 63.**

## Sec.21 Expenses for household and dependent care services necessary for gainful employment

### (a) Allowance of credit

#### (1) In general

In the case of an individual for which there are 1 or more qualifying individuals (as defined in subsection (b)(1)) with respect to such individual, there shall be allowed as a credit against the tax imposed by this chapter for the taxable year an amount equal to the applicable percentage of the employment-related expenses (as defined in subsection (b)(2)) paid by such individual during the taxable year.

#### (2) Applicable percentage defined

For purposes of paragraph (1), the term "applicable percentage" means 35 percent reduced (but not below 20 percent) by 1 percentage point for each $2,000 (or fraction thereof) by which the taxpayer's adjusted gross income for the taxable year exceeds $15,000.

### (b) Definitions of qualifying individual and employment-related expenses

For purposes of this section-

#### (1) Qualifying individual

The term "qualifying individual" means-

(A) a dependent of the taxpayer (as defined in section 152(a)(1)) who has not attained age 13,

(B) a dependent of the taxpayer (as defined in section 152, determined without regard to subsections (b)(1), (b)(2), and (d)(1)(B)) who is physically or mentally incapable of caring for himself or herself and who has the same principal place of abode as the taxpayer for more than one-half of such taxable year, or

(C) the spouse of the taxpayer, if the spouse is physically or mentally incapable of caring for himself or herself and who has the same principal place of abode as the taxpayer for more than one-half of such taxable year.

**(2) Employment-related expenses**

**(A) In general**

The term "employment-related expenses" means amounts paid for the following expenses, but only if such expenses are incurred to enable the taxpayer to be gainfully employed for any period for which there are 1 or more qualifying individuals with respect to the taxpayer:

(i) expenses for household services, and

(ii) expenses for the care of a qualifying individual.

Such term shall not include any amount paid for services outside the taxpayer's household at a camp where the qualifying individual stays overnight.

### (B) Exception

Employment-related expenses described in subparagraph (A) which are incurred for services outside the taxpayer's household shall be taken into account only if incurred for the care of-

(i) a qualifying individual described in paragraph (1)(A), or

(ii) a qualifying individual (not described in paragraph (1)(A)) who regularly spends at least 8 hours each day in the taxpayer's household.

### (C) Dependent care centers

Employment-related expenses described in subparagraph (A) which are incurred for services provided outside the taxpayer's household by a dependent care center (as defined in subparagraph (D)) shall be taken into account only if-

(i) such center complies with all applicable laws and regulations of a State or unit of local government, and

(ii) the requirements of subparagraph (B) are met.

### (D) Dependent care center defined

For purposes of this paragraph, the term "dependent care center" means any facility which-

(i) provides care for more than six individuals (other than individuals who reside at the facility), and

(ii) receives a fee, payment, or grant for providing services for any of the individuals (regardless of whether such facility is operated for profit).

## (c) Dollar limit on amount creditable

The amount of the employment-related expenses incurred during any taxable year which may be taken into account under subsection (a) shall not exceed-

(1) $3,000 if there is 1 qualifying individual with respect to the taxpayer for such taxable year, or

(2) $6,000 if there are 2 or more qualifying individuals with respect to the taxpayer for such taxable year.

The amount determined under paragraph (1) or (2) (whichever is applicable) shall be reduced by the aggregate amount excludable from gross income under section 129 for the taxable year.

## (d) Earned income limitation

### (1) In general

Except as otherwise provided in this subsection, the amount of the employment-related expenses incurred during any taxable year which may be taken into account under subsection (a) shall not exceed-

(A) in the case of an individual who is not married at the close of such year, such individual's earned income for such year, or

(B) in the case of an individual who is married at the close of such year, the lesser of such individual's earned income or the earned income of his spouse for such year.

### (2) Special rule for spouse who is a student or incapable of caring for himself

In the case of a spouse who is a student or a qualifying individual described in subsection (b)(1)(C), for purposes of paragraph (1), such spouse shall be deemed for each month during which such spouse is a full-time student at an educational institution, or is such a qualifying individual, to be gainfully employed and to have earned income of not less than-

(A) $250 if subsection (c)(1) applies for the taxable year, or

(B) $500 if subsection (c)(2) applies for the taxable year.

In the case of any husband and wife, this paragraph shall apply with respect to only one spouse for any one month.

### (e) Special rules

209

For purposes of this section-

### (1) Place of abode

An individual shall not be treated as having the same principal place of abode of the taxpayer if at any time during the taxable year of the taxpayer the relationship between the individual and the taxpayer is in violation of local law.

### (2) Married couples must file joint return

If the taxpayer is married at the close of the taxable year, the credit shall be allowed under subsection (a) only if the taxpayer and his spouse file a joint return for the taxable year.

### (3) Marital status

An individual legally separated from his spouse under a decree of divorce or of separate maintenance shall not be considered as married.

### (4) Certain married individuals living apart

If-

(A) an individual who is married and who files a separate return-

(i) maintains as his home a household which constitutes for more than one-half of the taxable year the principal place of abode of a qualifying individual, and

(ii) furnishes over half of the cost of maintaining such household during the taxable year, and

(B) during the last 6 months of such taxable year such individual's spouse is not a member of such household,

such individual shall not be considered as married.

**(5) Special dependency test in case of divorced parents, etc.**

If-

(A) section 152(e) applies to any child with respect to any calendar year, and

(B) such child is under the age of 13 or is physically or mentally incapable of caring for himself,

in the case of any taxable year beginning in such calendar year, such child shall be treated as a qualifying individual described in subparagraph (A) or (B) of subsection (b)(1)(whichever is appropriate) with respect to the custodial parent (as defined in section 152(e)(4)(A)), and shall not be treated as a qualifying individual with respect to the noncustodial parent.

**(6) Payments to related individuals**

No credit shall be allowed under subsection (a) for any amount paid by the taxpayer to an individual-

(A) with respect to whom, for the taxable year, a deduction under section 151(c)(relating to deduction

211

for personal exemptions for dependents) is allowable either to the taxpayer or his spouse, or

(B) who is a child of the taxpayer (within the meaning of section 152(f)(1)) who has not attained the age of 19 at the close of the taxable year.

For purposes of this paragraph, the term "taxable year" means the taxable year of the taxpayer in which the service is performed.

### (7) Student

The term "student" means an individual who during each of 5 calendar months during the taxable year is a full-time student at an educational organization.

### (8) Educational organization

The term "educational organization" means an educational organization described in section 170(b)(1)(A)(ii).

### (9) Identifying information required with respect to service provider

No credit shall be allowed under subsection (a) for any amount paid to any person unless-

(A) the name, address, and taxpayer identification number of such person are included on the return claiming the credit, or

(B) if such person is an organization described in section 501(c)(3) and exempt from tax under section 501(a), the name and address of such person are included on the return claiming the credit.

In the case of a failure to provide the information required under the preceding sentence, the preceding sentence shall not apply if it is shown that the taxpayer exercised due diligence in attempting to provide the information so required.

**(10) Identifying information required with respect to qualifying individuals**

No credit shall be allowed under this section with respect to any qualifying individual unless the TIN of such individual is included on the return claiming the credit.

**(f) Regulations**

The Secretary shall prescribe such regulations as may be necessary to carry out the purposes of this section.

### Sec.24 Child tax credit

#### (a) Allowance of credit

There shall be allowed as a credit against the tax imposed by this chapter for the taxable year with respect to each qualifying child of the taxpayer for which the taxpayer is allowed a deduction under section 151 an amount equal to $1,000.

#### (b) Limitations

#### (1) Limitation based on adjusted gross income

The amount of the credit allowable under subsection (a) shall be reduced (but not below zero) by $50 for each $1,000 (or fraction thereof) by which the taxpayer's modified adjusted gross income exceeds the threshold amount. For purposes of the preceding sentence, the term "modified adjusted gross income" means adjusted gross income increased by any amount excluded from gross income under section 911, 931, or 933.

#### (2) Threshold amount

For purposes of paragraph (1), the term "threshold amount" means-

(A) $110,000 in the case of a joint return,

(B) $75,000 in the case of an individual who is not married, and

(C) $55,000 in the case of a married individual filing a separate return.

For purposes of this paragraph, marital status shall be determined under section 7703.

## (c) Qualifying child

For purposes of this section-

### (1) In general

The term "qualifying child" means a qualifying child of the taxpayer (as defined in section 152(c)) who has not attained age 17.

### (2) Exception for certain noncitizens

The term "qualifying child" shall not include any individual who would not be a dependent if subparagraph (A) of section 152(b)(3) were applied without regard to all that follows "resident of the United States".

## (d) Portion of credit refundable

### (1) In general

The aggregate credits allowed to a taxpayer under subpart C shall be increased by the lesser of-

(A) the credit which would be allowed under this section without regard to this subsection and the limitation under section 26(a) or

(B) the amount by which the aggregate amount of credits allowed by this subpart (determined without

216

regard to this subsection) would increase if the limitation imposed by section 26(a) were increased by the greater of-

(i) 15 percent of so much of the taxpayer's earned income (within the meaning of section 32) which is taken into account in computing taxable income for the taxable year as exceeds $3,000, or

(ii) in the case of a taxpayer with 3 or more qualifying children, the excess (if any) of-

(I) the taxpayer's social security taxes for the taxable year, over

(II) the credit allowed under section 32 for the taxable year.

The amount of the credit allowed under this subsection shall not be treated as a credit allowed under this subpart and shall reduce the amount of credit otherwise allowable under subsection (a) without regard to section 26(a). For purposes of subparagraph (B), any amount excluded from gross income by reason of section 112 shall be treated as earned income which is taken into account in computing taxable income for the taxable year.

**(2) Social security taxes**

For purposes of paragraph (1)-

**(A) In general**

The term "social security taxes" means, with respect to any taxpayer for any taxable year-

(i) the amount of the taxes imposed by sections 3101 and 3201(a) on amounts received by the taxpayer during the calendar year in which the taxable year begins,

(ii) 50 percent of the taxes imposed by section 1401 on the self-employment income of the taxpayer for the taxable year, and

(iii) 50 percent of the taxes imposed by section 3211(a) on amounts received by the taxpayer during the calendar year in which the taxable year begins.

**(B) Coordination with special refund of social security taxes**

The term "social security taxes" shall not include any taxes to the extent the taxpayer is entitled to a special refund of such taxes under section 6413(c).

**(C) Special rule**

Any amounts paid pursuant to an agreement under section 3121(l)(relating to agreements entered into by American employers with respect to foreign affiliates) which are equivalent to the taxes referred to in subparagraph (A)(i) shall be treated as taxes referred to in such subparagraph.

**[(3), (4) Repealed. <u>Pub. L. 114–113, div. Q, title I, §101(b), Dec. 18, 2015, 129 Stat. 3044</u> ]**

**(5) Exception for taxpayers excluding foreign earned income**

Paragraph (1) shall not apply to any taxpayer for any taxable year if such taxpayer elects to exclude any amount from gross income under section 911 for such taxable year.

## (e) Identification requirements

### (1) Qualifying child identification requirement

No credit shall be allowed under this section to a taxpayer with respect to any qualifying child unless the taxpayer includes the name and taxpayer identification number of such qualifying child on the return of tax for the taxable year and such taxpayer identification number was issued on or before the due date for filing such return.

### (2) Taxpayer identification requirement

No credit shall be allowed under this section if the identifying number of the taxpayer was issued after the due date for filing the return for the taxable year.

## (f) Taxable year must be full taxable year

Except in the case of a taxable year closed by reason of the death of the taxpayer, no credit shall be allowable under this section in the case of a taxable year covering a period of less than 12 months.

## (g) Restrictions on taxpayers who improperly claimed credit in prior year

### (1) Taxpayers making prior fraudulent or reckless claims

#### (A) In general

No credit shall be allowed under this section for any taxable year in the disallowance period.

## (B) Disallowance period

For purposes of subparagraph (A), the disallowance period is-

(i) the period of 10 taxable years after the most recent taxable year for which there was a final determination that the taxpayer's claim of credit under this section was due to fraud, and

(ii) the period of 2 taxable years after the most recent taxable year for which there was a final determination that the taxpayer's claim of credit under this section was due to reckless or intentional disregard of rules and regulations (but not due to fraud).

## (2) Taxpayers making improper prior claims

In the case of a taxpayer who is denied credit under this section for any taxable year as a result of the deficiency procedures under subchapter B of chapter 63, no credit shall be allowed under this section for any subsequent taxable year unless the taxpayer provides such information as the Secretary may require to demonstrate eligibility for such credit.

## Sec.32 Earned income

### (a) Allowance of credit

#### (1) In general

In the case of an eligible individual, there shall be allowed as a credit against the tax imposed by this subtitle for the taxable year an amount equal to the credit percentage of so much of the taxpayer's earned income for the taxable year as does not exceed the earned income amount.

#### (2) Limitation

The amount of the credit allowable to a taxpayer under paragraph (1) for any taxable year shall not exceed the excess (if any) of-

(A) the credit percentage of the earned income amount, over

(B) the phase-out percentage of so much of the adjusted gross income (or, if greater, the earned income) of the taxpayer for the taxable year as exceeds the phase-out amount.

### (b) Percentages and amounts

For purposes of subsection (a)-

#### (1) Percentages

The credit percentage and the phase-out percentage shall be determined as follows:

| In the case of an eligible individual with: | The credit percentage is: | The phase-out percentage is: |
|---|---|---|
| 1 qualifying child | 34 | 15.98 |
| 2 qualifying children | 40 | 21.06 |
| 3 or more qualifying children | 45 | 21.06 |
| No qualifying children | 7.65 | 7.65 |

## (2) Amounts

### (A) In general

Subject to subparagraph (B), the earned income amount and the phase-out amount shall be determined as follows:

| In the case of an eligible individual with: | The earned income amount is: | The phase-out amount is: |
|---|---|---|
| 1 qualifying child | $6,330 | $11,610 |
| 2 qualifying children | $8,890 | $11,610 |
| No qualifying children | $4,220 | $5,280 |

### (B) Joint returns

#### (i) In general

In the case of a joint return filed by an eligible individual and such individual's spouse, the phase-out amount determined under subparagraph (A) shall be increased by $5,000.

### (ii) Inflation adjustment

In the case of any taxable year beginning after 2015, the $5,000 amount in clause (i) shall be increased by an amount equal to-

(I) such dollar amount, multiplied by

(II) the cost of living adjustment determined under section 1(f)(3) for the calendar year in which the taxable year begins determined by substituting "calendar year 2008" for "calendar year 1992" in subparagraph (B) thereof.

### (iii) Rounding

Subparagraph (A) of subsection (j)(2) shall apply after taking into account any increase under clause (ii).

### (c) Definitions and special rules

For purposes of this section-

### (1) Eligible individual

### (A) In general

The term "eligible individual" means-

(i) any individual who has a qualifying child for the taxable year, or

(ii) any other individual who does not have a qualifying child for the taxable year, if-

(I) such individual's principal place of abode is in the United States for more than one-half of such taxable year,

(II) such individual (or, if the individual is married, either the individual or the individual's spouse) has attained age 25 but not attained age 65 before the close of the taxable year, and

(III) such individual is not a dependent for whom a deduction is allowable under section 151 to another taxpayer for any taxable year beginning in the same calendar year as such taxable year.

For purposes of the preceding sentence, marital status shall be determined under section 7703.

## (B) Qualifying child ineligible

If an individual is the qualifying child of a taxpayer for any taxable year of such taxpayer beginning in a calendar year, such individual shall not be treated as an eligible individual for any taxable year of such individual beginning in such calendar year.

## (C) Exception for individual claiming benefits under section 911

The term "eligible individual" does not include any individual who claims the benefits of section 911 (relating to citizens or residents living abroad) for the taxable year.

## (D) Limitation on eligibility of nonresident aliens

The term "eligible individual" shall not include any individual who is a nonresident alien individual for any portion of the taxable year unless such individual is treated for such taxable year as a resident of the United States for purposes of this chapter by reason of an election under subsection (g) or (h) of section 6013.

### (E) Identification number requirement

No credit shall be allowed under this section to an eligible individual who does not include on the return of tax for the taxable year-

(i) such individual's taxpayer identification number, and

(ii) if the individual is married (within the meaning of section 7703), the taxpayer identification number of such individual's spouse.

### (F) Individuals who do not include TIN, etc., of any qualifying child

No credit shall be allowed under this section to any eligible individual who has one or more qualifying children if no qualifying child of such individual is taken into account under subsection (b) by reason of paragraph (3)(D).

### (2) Earned income

(A) The term "earned income" means-

(i) wages, salaries, tips, and other employee compensation, but only if such amounts are

includible in gross income for the taxable
year, plus

(ii) the amount of the taxpayer's net earnings
from self-employment for the taxable year
(within the meaning of section 1402(a)), but
such net earnings shall be determined with
regard to the deduction allowed to the
taxpayer by section 164(f).

(B) For purposes of subparagraph (A)-

(i) the earned income of an individual shall be
computed without regard to any community
property laws,

(ii) no amount received as a pension or
annuity shall be taken into account,

(iii) no amount to which section 871(a) applies
(relating to income of nonresident alien
individuals not connected with United States
business) shall be taken into account,

(iv) no amount received for services provided
by an individual while the individual is an
inmate at a penal institution shall be taken into
account,

(v) no amount described in subparagraph (A)
received for service performed in work
activities as defined in paragraph (4) or (7) of
section 407(d) of the Social Security Act to
which the taxpayer is assigned under any State
program under part A of title IV of such Act

shall be taken into account, but only to the extent such amount is subsidized under such State program, and

(vi) a taxpayer may elect to treat amounts excluded from gross income by reason of section 112 as earned income.

## (3) Qualifying child

### (A) In general

The term "qualifying child" means a qualifying child of the taxpayer (as defined in section 152(c), determined without regard to paragraph (1)(D) thereof and section 152(e)).

### (B) Married individual

The term "qualifying child" shall not include an individual who is married as of the close of the taxpayer's taxable year unless the taxpayer is entitled to a deduction under section 151 for such taxable year with respect to such individual (or would be so entitled but for section 152(e)).

### (C) Place of abode

For purposes of subparagraph (A), the requirements of section 152(c)(1)(B) shall be met only if the principal place of abode is in the United States.

## (D) Identification requirements

### (i) In general

A qualifying child shall not be taken into account under subsection (b) unless the taxpayer includes the name, age, and TIN of the qualifying child on the return of tax for the taxable year.

### (ii) Other methods

The Secretary may prescribe other methods for providing the information described in clause (i).

## (4) Treatment of military personnel stationed outside the United States

For purposes of paragraphs (1)(A)(ii)(I) and (3)(C), the principal place of abode of a member of the Armed Forces of the United States shall be treated as in the United States during any period during which such member is stationed outside the United States while serving on extended active duty with the Armed Forces of the United States. For purposes of the preceding sentence, the term "extended active duty" means any period of active duty pursuant to a call or order to such duty for a period in excess of 90 days or for an indefinite period.

## (d) Married individuals

In the case of an individual who is married (within the meaning of section 7703), this section shall apply only if a joint return is filed for the taxable year under section 6013.

**(e) Taxable year must be full taxable year**

Except in the case of a taxable year closed by reason of the death of the taxpayer, no credit shall be allowable under this section in the case of a taxable year covering a period of less than 12 months.

**(f) Amount of credit to be determined under tables**

**(1) In general**

The amount of the credit allowed by this section shall be determined under tables prescribed by the Secretary.

**(2) Requirements for tables**

The tables prescribed under paragraph (1) shall reflect the provisions of subsections (a) and (b) and shall have income brackets of not greater than $50 each-

> (A) for earned income between $0 and the amount of earned income at which the credit is phased out under subsection (b), and

> (B) for adjusted gross income between the dollar amount at which the phase-out begins under subsection (b) and the amount of adjusted gross income at which the credit is phased out under subsection (b).

**[(g) Repealed. Pub. L. 111–226, title II, §219(a)(2), Aug. 10, 2010, 124 Stat. 2403]**

**[(h) Repealed. Pub. L. 107–16, title III, §303(c), June 7, 2001, 115 Stat. 55]**

### (i) Denial of credit for individuals having excessive investment income

### (1) In general

No credit shall be allowed under subsection (a) for the taxable year if the aggregate amount of disqualified income of the taxpayer for the taxable year exceeds $2,200.

### (2) Disqualified income

For purposes of paragraph (1), the term "disqualified income" means-

(A) interest or dividends to the extent includible in gross income for the taxable year,

(B) interest received or accrued during the taxable year which is exempt from tax imposed by      this chapter,

(C) the excess (if any) of-

(i) gross income from rents or royalties not derived in the ordinary course of a trade or   business, over

(ii) the sum of-

(I) the deductions (other than interest) which are clearly and directly allocable to such gross income, plus

(II) interest deductions properly allocable to such gross income,

(D) the capital gain net income (as defined in section 1222) of the taxpayer for such taxable year, and

(E) the excess (if any) of-

> (i) the aggregate income from all passive activities for the taxable year (determined without regard to any amount included in earned income under subsection (c)(2) or described in a preceding subparagraph), over

> (ii) the aggregate losses from all passive activities for the taxable year (as so determined).

For purposes of subparagraph (E), the term "passive activity" has the meaning given such term by section 469.

## (j) Inflation adjustments

### (1) In general

In the case of any taxable year beginning after 1996, each of the dollar amounts in subsections (b)(2) and (i)(1) shall be increased by an amount equal to-

(A) such dollar amount, multiplied by

(B) the cost-of-living adjustment determined under section 1(f)(3) for the calendar year in which the taxable year begins, determined-

> (i) in the case of amounts in subsections (b)(2)(A) and (i)(1), by substituting "calendar year 1995" for

"calendar year 1992" in subparagraph (B) thereof, and

(ii) in the case of the $3,000 amount in subsection (b)(2)(B)(iii), by substituting "calendar year 2007" for "calendar year 1992" in subparagraph (B) of such section 1.

## (2) Rounding

### (A) In general

If any dollar amount in subsection (b)(2)(A)(after being increased under subparagraph (B) thereof), after being increased under paragraph (1), is not a multiple of $10, such dollar amount shall be rounded to the nearest multiple of $10.

### (B) Disqualified income threshold amount

If the dollar amount in subsection (i)(1), after being increased under paragraph (1), is not a multiple of $50, such amount shall be rounded to the next lowest multiple of $50.

## (k) Restrictions on taxpayers who improperly claimed credit in prior year

### (1) Taxpayers making prior fraudulent or reckless claims

### (A) In general

No credit shall be allowed under this section for any taxable year in the disallowance period.

### (B) Disallowance period

For purposes of paragraph (1), the disallowance period is-

  (i) the period of 10 taxable years after the most recent taxable year for which there was a final determination that the taxpayer's claim of credit under this section was due to fraud, and

  (ii) the period of 2 taxable years after the most recent taxable year for which there was a final determination that the taxpayer's claim of credit under this section was due to reckless or intentional disregard of rules and regulations (but not due to fraud).

## (2) Taxpayers making improper prior claims

In the case of a taxpayer who is denied credit under this section for any taxable year as a result of the deficiency procedures under subchapter B of chapter 63, no credit shall be allowed under this section for any subsequent taxable year unless the taxpayer provides such information as the Secretary may require to demonstrate eligibility for such credit.

## (l) Coordination with certain means-tested programs

For purposes of-

(1) the United States Housing Act of 1937,

(2) title V of the Housing Act of 1949,

(3) section 101 of the Housing and Urban Development Act of 1965,

(4) sections 221(d)(3), 235, and 236 of the National Housing Act, and

(5) the Food and Nutrition Act of 2008,

any refund made to an individual (or the spouse of an individual) by reason of this section, and any payment made to such individual (or such spouse) by an employer under section 3507,[1] shall not be treated as income (and shall not be taken into account in determining resources for the month of its receipt and the following month).

**(m) Identification numbers**

Solely for purposes of subsections (c)(1)(E) and (c)(3)(D), a taxpayer identification number means a social security number issued to an individual by the Social Security Administration (other than a social security number issued pursuant to clause (II)(or that portion of clause (III) that relates to clause (II)) of section 205(c)(2)(B)(i) of the Social Security Act) on or before the due date for filing the return for the taxable year.

## Sec.151 Allowance of deductions for personal exemptions

### (a) Allowance of deductions

In the case of an individual, the exemptions provided by this section shall be allowed as deductions in computing taxable income.

### (b) Taxpayer and spouse

An exemption of the exemption amount for the taxpayer; and an additional exemption of the exemption amount for the spouse of the taxpayer if a joint return is not made by the taxpayer and his spouse, and if the spouse, for the calendar year in which the taxable year of the taxpayer begins, has no gross income and is not the dependent of another taxpayer.

### (c) Additional exemption for dependents

An exemption of the exemption amount for each individual who is a dependent (as defined in section 152) of the taxpayer for the taxable year.

### (d) Exemption amount

For purposes of this section-

#### (1) In general

Except as otherwise provided in this subsection, the term "exemption amount" means $2,000.

#### (2) Exemption amount disallowed in case of certain dependents

In the case of an individual with respect to whom a deduction under this section is allowable to another taxpayer for a taxable year beginning in the calendar year in which the individual's taxable year begins, the exemption amount applicable to such individual for such individual's taxable year shall be zero.

### (3) Phase-out

### (A) In general

In the case of any taxpayer whose adjusted gross income for the taxable year exceeds the applicable amount in effect under section 68(b), the exemption amount shall be reduced by the applicable percentage.

### (B) Applicable percentage

For purposes of subparagraph (A), the term "applicable percentage" means 2 percentage points for each $2,500 (or fraction thereof) by which the taxpayer's adjusted gross income for the taxable year exceeds the applicable amount in effect under section 68(b). In the case of a married individual filing a separate return, the preceding sentence shall be applied by substituting "$1,250" for "$2,500". In no event shall the applicable percentage exceed 100 percent.

### (C) Coordination with other provisions

The provisions of this paragraph shall not apply for purposes of determining whether a deduction under this section with respect to any individual is allowable to another taxpayer for any taxable year.

### (4) Inflation adjustment

In the case of any taxable year beginning in a calendar year after 1989, the dollar amount contained in paragraph (1) shall be increased by an amount equal to-

      (A) such dollar amount, multiplied by

      (B) the cost-of-living adjustment determined under section 1(f)(3) for the calendar year in which the taxable year begins, by substituting "calendar year 1988" for "calendar year 1992" in subparagraph (B) thereof.

### (e) Identifying information required

No exemption shall be allowed under this section with respect to any individual unless the TIN of such individual is included on the return claiming the exemption.

## Sec.152 Dependent defined

### (a) In general

For purposes of this subtitle, the term "dependent" means-

>(1) a qualifying child, or

>(2) a qualifying relative.

### (b) Exceptions

For purposes of this section-

#### (1) Dependents ineligible

If an individual is a dependent of a taxpayer for any taxable year of such taxpayer beginning in a calendar year, such individual shall be treated as having no dependents for any taxable year of such individual beginning in such calendar year.

#### (2) Married dependents

An individual shall not be treated as a dependent of a taxpayer under subsection (a) if such individual has made a joint return with the individual's spouse under section 6013 for the taxable year beginning in the calendar year in which the taxable year of the taxpayer begins.

### (3) Citizens or nationals of other countries

### (A) In general

The term "dependent" does not include an individual who is not a citizen or national of the United States unless such individual is a resident of the United States or a country contiguous to the United States.

### (B) Exception for adopted child

Subparagraph (A) shall not exclude any child of a taxpayer (within the meaning of subsection (f)(1)(B)) from the definition of "dependent" if-

(i) for the taxable year of the taxpayer, the child has the same principal place of abode as the taxpayer and is a member of the taxpayer's household, and

(ii) the taxpayer is a citizen or national of the United States.

### (c) Qualifying child

For purposes of this section-

### (1) In general

The term "qualifying child" means, with respect to any taxpayer for any taxable year, an individual-

(A) who bears a relationship to the taxpayer described in paragraph (2),

(B) who has the same principal place of abode as the taxpayer for more than one-half of such taxable year,

(C) who meets the age requirements of paragraph (3),

(D) who has not provided over one-half of such individual's own support for the calendar year in which the taxable year of the taxpayer begins, and

(E) who has not filed a joint return (other than only for a claim of refund) with the individual's spouse under section 6013 for the taxable year beginning in the calendar year in which the taxable year of the taxpayer begins.

## (2) Relationship

For purposes of paragraph (1)(A), an individual bears a relationship to the taxpayer described in this paragraph if such individual is-

(A) a child of the taxpayer or a descendant of such a child, or

(B) a brother, sister, stepbrother, or stepsister of the taxpayer or a descendant of any such relative.

## (3) Age requirements

## (A) In general

For purposes of paragraph (1)(C), an individual meets the requirements of this paragraph if such individual is younger than the taxpayer claiming such individual as a qualifying child and-

(i) has not attained the age of 19 as of the close of the calendar year in which the taxable year of the taxpayer begins, or

(ii) is a student who has not attained the age of 24 as of the close of such calendar year.

### (B) Special rule for disabled

In the case of an individual who is permanently and totally disabled (as defined in section 22(e)(3)) at any time during such calendar year, the requirements of subparagraph (A) shall be treated as met with respect to such individual.

### (4) Special rule relating to 2 or more who can claim the same qualifying child

### (A) In general

Except as provided in subparagraphs (B) and (C), if (but for this paragraph) an individual may be claimed as a qualifying child by 2 or more taxpayers for a taxable year beginning in the same calendar year, such individual shall be treated as the qualifying child of the taxpayer who is-

(i) a parent of the individual, or

(ii) if clause (i) does not apply, the taxpayer with the highest adjusted gross income for such taxable year.

### (B) More than 1 parent claiming qualifying child

If the parents claiming any qualifying child do not file a joint return together, such child shall be treated as the qualifying child of-

(i) the parent with whom the child resided for the longest period of time during the taxable year, or

(ii) if the child resides with both parents for the same amount of time during such taxable year, the parent with the highest adjusted gross income.

### (C) No parent claiming qualifying child

If the parents of an individual may claim such individual as a qualifying child but no parent so claims the individual, such individual may be claimed as the qualifying child of another taxpayer but only if the adjusted gross income of such taxpayer is higher than the highest adjusted gross income of any parent of the individual.

### (d) Qualifying relative

For purposes of this section-

### (1) In general

The term "qualifying relative" means, with respect to any taxpayer for any taxable year, an individual-

(A) who bears a relationship to the taxpayer described in paragraph (2),

(B) whose gross income for the calendar year in which such taxable year begins is less than the exemption amount (as defined in section 151(d)),

(C) with respect to whom the taxpayer provides over one-half of the individual's support for the calendar year in which such taxable year begins, and

(D) who is not a qualifying child of such taxpayer or of any other taxpayer for any taxable year beginning in the calendar year in which such taxable year begins.

## (2) Relationship

For purposes of paragraph (1)(A), an individual bears a relationship to the taxpayer described in this paragraph if the individual is any of the following with respect to the taxpayer:

(A) A child or a descendant of a child.

(B) A brother, sister, stepbrother, or stepsister.

(C) The father or mother, or an ancestor of either.

(D) A stepfather or stepmother.

(E) A son or daughter of a brother or sister of the taxpayer.

(F) A brother or sister of the father or mother of the taxpayer.

(G) A son-in-law, daughter-in-law, father-in-law, mother-in-law, brother-in-law, or sister-in-law.

(H) An individual (other than an individual who at any time during the taxable year was the spouse, determined without regard to section 7703, of the taxpayer) who, for the taxable year of the taxpayer, has the same principal place of abode as the taxpayer and is a member of the taxpayer's household.

**(3) Special rule relating to multiple support agreements**

For purposes of paragraph (1)(C), over one-half of the support of an individual for a calendar year shall be treated as received from the taxpayer if-

(A) no one person contributed over one-half of such support,

(B) over one-half of such support was received from 2 or more persons each of whom, but for the fact that any such person alone did not contribute over one-half of such support, would have been entitled to claim such individual as a dependent for a taxable year beginning in such calendar year,

(C) the taxpayer contributed over 10 percent of such support, and

(D) each person described in subparagraph (B)(other than the taxpayer) who contributed over 10 percent of such support files a written declaration (in such manner and form as the Secretary may by regulations prescribe) that such person will not claim such individual as a dependent for any taxable year beginning in such calendar year.

### (4) Special rule relating to income of handicapped dependents

### (A) In general

For purposes of paragraph (1)(B), the gross income of an individual who is permanently and totally disabled (as defined in section 22(e)(3)) at any time during the taxable year shall not include income attributable to services performed by the individual at a sheltered workshop if-

> (i) the availability of medical care at such workshop is the principal reason for the individual's presence there, and

> (ii) the income arises solely from activities at such workshop which are incident to such medical care.

### (B) Sheltered workshop defined

For purposes of subparagraph (A), the term "sheltered workshop" means a school-

> (i) which provides special instruction or training designed to alleviate the disability of the individual, and

> (ii) which is operated by an organization described in section 501(c)(3) and exempt from tax under section 501(a), or by a State, a possession of the United States, any political subdivision of any of the

foregoing, the United States, or the District of Columbia.

## (5) Special rules for support

For purposes of this subsection-

(A) payments to a spouse which are includible in the gross income of such spouse under section 71 or 682 shall not be treated as a payment by the payor spouse for the support of any dependent, and

(B) in the case of the remarriage of a parent, support of a child received from the parent's spouse shall be treated as received from the parent.

## (e) Special rule for divorced parents, etc.

## (1) In general

Notwithstanding subsection (c)(1)(B), (c)(4), or (d)(1)(C), if-

(A) a child receives over one-half of the child's support during the calendar year from the child's parents-

(i) who are divorced or legally separated under a decree of divorce or separate maintenance,

(ii) who are separated under a written separation agreement, or

(iii) who live apart at all times during the last 6 months of the calendar year, and-

(B) such child is in the custody of 1 or both of the child's parents for more than one-half of the calendar year, such child shall be treated as being the qualifying child or qualifying relative of the noncustodial parent for a calendar year if the requirements described in paragraph (2) or (3) are met.

### (B) Qualified pre-1985 instrument

For purposes of this paragraph, the term "qualified pre-1985 instrument" means any decree of divorce or separate maintenance or written agreement-

(i) which is executed before January 1, 1985,

(ii) which on such date contains the provision described in subparagraph (A)(i), and

(iii) which is not modified on or after such date in a modification which expressly provides that this paragraph shall not apply to such decree or agreement.

### (2) Exception where custodial parent releases claim to exemption for the year

For purposes of paragraph (1), the requirements described in this paragraph are met with respect to any calendar year if-

(A) the custodial parent signs a written declaration (in such manner and form as the Secretary may by regulations prescribe) that such custodial parent will not claim such child as a dependent for any taxable year beginning in such calendar year, and

(B) the noncustodial parent attaches such written declaration to the noncustodial parent's return for the taxable year beginning during such calendar year.

### (3) Exception for certain pre-1985 instruments

### (A) In general

For purposes of paragraph (1), the requirements described in this paragraph are met with respect to any calendar year if-

(i) a qualified pre-1985 instrument between the parents applicable to the taxable year beginning in such calendar year provides that the noncustodial parent shall be entitled to any deduction allowable under section 151 for such child, and

(ii) the noncustodial parent provides at least $600 for the support of such child during such calendar year.

For purposes of this subparagraph, amounts expended for the support of a child or children shall be treated as received from the noncustodial parent to the extent that such parent provided amounts for such support.

### (4) Custodial parent and noncustodial parent

For purposes of this subsection-

### (A) Custodial parent

The term "custodial parent" means the parent having custody for the greater portion of the calendar year.

### (B) Noncustodial parent

The term "noncustodial parent" means the parent who is not the custodial parent.

### (5) Exception for multiple-support agreement

This subsection shall not apply in any case where over one-half of the support of the child is treated as having been received from a taxpayer under the provision of subsection (d)(3).

### (6) Special rule for support received from new spouse of parent

For purposes of this subsection, in the case of the remarriage of a parent, support of a child received from the parent's spouse shall be treated as received from the parent.

### (f) Other definitions and rules

For purposes of this section-

### (1) Child defined

### (A) In general

The term "child" means an individual who is-

(i) a son, daughter, stepson, or stepdaughter of the taxpayer, or

(ii) an eligible foster child of the taxpayer.

### (B) Adopted child

In determining whether any of the relationships specified in subparagraph (A)(i) or paragraph (4) exists, a legally adopted individual of the taxpayer, or an individual who is lawfully placed with the taxpayer for legal adoption by the taxpayer, shall be treated as a child of such individual by blood.

### (C) Eligible foster child

For purposes of subparagraph (A)(ii), the term "eligible foster child" means an individual who is placed with the taxpayer by an authorized placement agency or by judgment, decree, or other order of any court of competent jurisdiction.

### (2) Student defined

The term "student" means an individual who during each of 5 calendar months during the calendar year in which the taxable year of the taxpayer begins-

(A) is a full-time student at an educational organization described in section 170(b)(1)(A)(ii), or

(B) is pursuing a full-time course of institutional on-farm training under the supervision of an accredited agent of an educational organization described in section 170(b)(1)(A)(ii) or of a State or political subdivision of a State.

### (3) Determination of household status

An individual shall not be treated as a member of the taxpayer's household if at any time during the taxable year of the taxpayer the relationship between such individual and the taxpayer is in violation of local law.

### (4) Brother and sister

The terms "brother" and "sister" include a brother or sister by the half blood.

### (5) Special support test in case of students

For purposes of subsections (c)(1)(D) and (d)(1)(C), in the case of an individual who is-

(A) a child of the taxpayer, and

(B) a student,

amounts received as scholarships for study at an educational organization described in section 170(b)(1)(A)(ii) shall not be taken into account.

### (6) Treatment of missing children

### (A) In general

Solely for the purposes referred to in subparagraph (B), a child of the taxpayer-

(i) who is presumed by law enforcement authorities to have been kidnapped by someone who is not a member of the family of such child or the taxpayer, and

(ii) who had, for the taxable year in which the kidnapping occurred, the same principal place of abode as the taxpayer for more than one-half of the portion of such year before the date of the kidnapping,

shall be treated as meeting the requirement of subsection (c)(1)(B) with respect to a taxpayer for all taxable years ending during the period that the child is kidnapped.

### (B) Purposes

Subparagraph (A) shall apply solely for purposes of determining-

(i) the deduction under section 151(c),

(ii) the credit under section 24 (relating to child tax credit),

(iii) whether an individual is a surviving spouse or a head of a household (as such terms are defined in section 2), and

(iv) the earned income credit under section 32.

### (C) Comparable treatment of certain qualifying relatives

For purposes of this section, a child of the taxpayer-

(i) who is presumed by law enforcement authorities to have been kidnapped by someone who is not a member of the family of such child or the taxpayer, and

(ii) who was (without regard to this paragraph) a qualifying relative of the taxpayer for the portion of the taxable year before the date of the kidnapping,

shall be treated as a qualifying relative of the taxpayer for all taxable years ending during the period that the child is kidnapped.

### (D) Termination of treatment

Subparagraphs (A) and (C) shall cease to apply as of the first taxable year of the taxpayer beginning after the calendar year in which there is a determination that the child is dead (or, if earlier, in which the child would have attained age 18).

### (7) Cross references

**For provision treating child as dependent of both parents for purposes of certain provisions, see sections 105(b), 132(h)(2)(B), and 213(d)(5).**

Applicable IRC Sections

## Published Articles

I have written several articles related to the topics covered in this book. I have listed them here with an Internet link or my email address. The Journal of Accountancy and the National Association of Tax Professionals (NATP), publisher of TAXPRO Journal and TAXPRO Monthly have granted permission to allow access to or share them.

| Title | Journal | Date | Pages | Internet Link |
|---|---|---|---|---|
| Tax Issues Facing a Surviving Spouse with co-author Mark Nielsen, CPA | Practical Tax Strategies | October 2017 | 34-39 | Contact me at my email of: hopkins@morningside.edu |
| Qualifying Child/Qualifying Relative-Tiebreaker rules for eligible persons | TAXPRO Monthly | May/June 2015 | 6-7 | Contact me at my email of: hopkins@morningside.edu |
| Head of Household-Legally married, but not | TAXPRO Journal | Spring 2015 | 34-37 | Contact me at my email of: hopkins@morningside.edu |
| Father Was Custodial Parent for Dependency Exemption and Earned Income Credit | Journal of Accountancy | Nov 2014 | 82 | http://www.journalofaccountancy.com/issues/2014/nov/custodial-parent.html |
| Dependency Exemption-Not Always A Clear Issue | TAXPRO Monthly | Jan 2014 | 1,3 | Contact me at my email of: hopkins@morningside.edu |
| Family Matters-A Closer Look at Qualifying Child-Qualifying Relative Matters | TAXPRO Journal | Summer 2011 | 14-18 | Contact me at my email of: hopkins@morningside.edu |
| Scholarships and Support | Journal of Accountancy | May 2011 | 56-57 | http://www.journalofaccountancy.com/issues/2011/may/20113902.html |
| Clarifying Head of Household Issues | CPA Journal | Oct 2011 | 42-46 | http://viewer.zmags.com/publication/261bb12d#/261bb12d/1, or contact me using the above email address. |
| Unrelated Child as a Qualifying Relative | Journal of Accountancy | Nov 2009 | 68 | http://www.journalofaccountancy.com/issues/2009/nov/20091989.html |
| Qualifying Child Definition Amended | Journal of Accountancy | Nov 2009 | 74 | http://www.journalofaccountancy.com/issues/2009/nov/qualifyingchild.html |

My article, Family Matters-a Closer look at Qualifying Child /Qualifying Relatives, is reprinted with permission of the National Association of Tax Professionals (NATP). It originally appeared in the Summer 2011 issue of the TaxPro Journal.

## Family Matters: A closer look at qualifying child and qualifying relative [sic]

By James M. Hopkins, CPA, MA

Effective with the Working Families Tax Relief Tax Act of 2004 (WFTRA), the rules for dependency exemptions were revised. This created two exemption categories—qualifying child and qualifying relative, which can be confusing at times, especially when several related individuals, but separate taxpayers, live in the same household for more than half of the year.

The tests for the exemption categories are:

### Qualifying Child (QC)
• Relationship test
• Full-time student or age test
• Residence/abode test
• Dependent provides less than half support
• No joint return with spouse, except for refund claim

### Qualifying Relative (QR)
• Relationship test
• Gross income less than exemption amount
• Residence/abode test for unrelated dependent
• Claimant provides over half of dependent's support
• Dependent is not a QC of any other taxpayer

Using examples, this article will discuss different aspects of these two tests, starting with a beginning set of facts, making various modifications to the beginning facts, and then reanalyzing the changed facts.

**Example 1**
Amber is 21, unmarried, lives with her parents, attends college full-time and does not provide more than half her support.
Amber meets all five of the QC tests. Her parents can claim her as a QC dependent. She is not a QR, since a dependent who is a QC cannot be a QR.

**Example 2**
The facts are the same as in Example 1, except that Amber has a two-year-old son, Lucas, who lived with her and her parents for the entire year.
Amber is a QC of her parents. Lucas would normally be Amber's QC, but he is also a QC of his grandparents. Because Amber is a QC of her parents, she cannot claim any dependents on her personal return. Lucas is a QC of the grandparents and is not Amber's QC or QR. The grandparents can claim the benefits of a QC for him. The benefits related to a QC are: (1) an exemption; (2) the child tax credit; (3) a head of household (HOH) filing status, if available; (4) an exclusion of child and dependent benefits from income/dependent care credit; and (5) the earned income credit, if such benefits are otherwise available. It's my conclusion that the special tiebreaker rules (discussed later) when a dependent is the QC of two or more persons do not apply in this situation, because Lucas is not Amber's QC, and she cannot claim any dependents on her return when claimed by her parents.
HOH filing status is probably not relevant in this case as Amber's parents, being married, would probably file as married filing jointly. It would be relevant if the household was provided by an unmarried parent (only one grandparent in the above example) for a child and grandchild.

Special rules apply when the parents of children are divorced, separated, never married, or living apart. These rules will be discussed after Example 4, below.

**Example 3**
Amber is 21, unmarried, lives with her parents and does not provide more than half her support. She has a two-year-old son, Lucas, who lived with her and her parents for the entire year. In this example, Amber is not a full-time student. Amber is not a QC of her parents, as she fails the full-time student/age test. If Amber can satisfy the four QR tests, her parents can claim her as a QR exemption. The key QR test is Amber's gross income for the year. This will be discussed in a later example. Lucas is not a QC of the mother if she is claimed as a dependent on her parents' return, because anyone claimed as a dependent on another tax return cannot claim any dependents. Accordingly, the grandparents can claim all benefits for Lucas if they are otherwise available. If the grandparents are ineligible for some of these benefits, such as an AGI that is too high for the earned income credit, Amber cannot claim any of them.

**Example 4**
The facts are the same as in Example 3, except Amber has gross income exceeding the personal exemption amount ($3,650 for 2010).
Amber is not a QC of her parents, because she fails the full-time student/age test. Nor is she a QR, because she fails the gross income test. Amber must file her own return claiming an exemption for herself. Lucas is a QC of both Amber and his grandparents. This requires the application of the tiebreaker rules, which assign the QC to Amber but allow her to give it to her parents if they have a higher AGI. This is a choice the taxpayers need to make prior to each party filing a tax return. The parents and Amber need to plan for who gets to claim Lucas as a QC. The QC benefits all accrue to the person claiming Lucas as an exemption. It may be

advantageous for Amber, depending on her earned income, to claim Lucas as a QC when the child tax credit, dependent care credit, exclusion of dependent care benefits excluded from income, exemption and earned income credit are considered. (See IRS Notice 2006-86, 2006-2 C.B. 680, effective for tax years beginning January 1, 2005, which states that a child is treated as the QC of only one taxpayer for all benefits mentioned above.) (Notice 2006-86 will be obsolete by the proposed regulations.)

Additional consideration for parents who are divorced, separated, never married, or live apart. Special rules of §152(e) apply to children of parents who fit into any of these categories. In most cases, a child of divorced/separated parents or parents who live apart is the QC of the custodial parent because of the residency test. However, the child can be treated as the QC of the noncustodial parent if four rules are satisfied. These rules require that: (1) the parents be divorced or legally separated under a divorce decree or separate maintenance agreement, or the parents live apart the last six months of the year; (2) the child is in the custody of one or both parents during the year; (3) the child received over half of his or her support for the year from the parents; and (4) the custodial parent (the mother in the above examples, since the father was not present in the household) consents to not claim the child as an exemption and for the child tax credit by signing Form 8332. The noncustodial parent must attach Form 8332 to his tax return. As a result, the noncustodial parent can claim the child as a dependent and for the child tax credit, but no other benefits, including head of household filing status. The custodial parent could claim the child for child and dependent care credit, earned income credit, dependent care benefits excluded from income and head of household (not an issue in the above examples, because the grandparents are married), if otherwise available, or allow her parents to claim such benefits if the parents' AGI is higher. (IRS Publication 17, Your Federal Income Tax 2010, p. 29–30, Examples 1 and 2, starting at the bottom of the page.) If Lucas's parents did not live apart during the last six months of the year, this provision is not available.

It is assumed the grandparents provided the cost of the residence in Examples 2 through 4 and over half the support for Amber and Lucas. Lucas's father and mother did not provide over half of the child's support; these rules did not apply in these examples. Tax advisors have to be aware of the application of the §152(e) rules to properly advise clients when they apply.

**Example 5**

In this example, Amber is not a full-time student and has gross income exceeding the personal exemption amount ($3,650 for 2010), but Lucas did not live with his mother for more than six months during the year; he lived with his grandparents for over six months during the year.

Amber is not a QC or QR of her parents, as she fails the full-time student/age test for a QC, and she fails the QR gross income test. Lucas cannot be Amber's QC since Lucas did not live with her for more than six months during the tax year. In order for Lucas to qualify as a QR of his mother, he cannot be a QC of any other taxpayer, which is not satisfied in this case. As a result, Lucas does not qualify as Amber's QR because he is a QC of the grandparents. The grandparents are entitled to all the benefits related to the QC exemption for Lucas, provided they otherwise qualify for them. Amber cannot claim any benefits for Lucas, and would have to file as single because she is unmarried. The grandparents are the only taxpayers who can claim Lucas as a QC. The tiebreaker rules do not apply.

The Additional Consideration for children of parents who were never married, divorced, or separated mentioned below Example 4 do not apply because Amber's child was not in the care of either parent for more than half the year, and Lucas's parents did not provide more than half of his support. If the mother provided over half of Lucas's support, Lucas would not be her QR, as he is a QC of the grandparents.

## Example 6

Amber is 21, lives with her parents and does not provide more than half her support. She has a two-year-old son, Lucas, who lived with her and her parents for the entire year. Amber is not a full-time student and has gross income exceeding the personal exemption amount ($3,650 for 2010). In this example, Lucas's 23-year-old father, Adam, lives with Amber's parents as well. Amber and Adam are not married. Lucas's parents each earn more than $3,650 for the year and neither is a full-time student. A majority of the household expenses are paid by Amber's parents, which prevents Adam and Amber from claiming head of household filing status. With the addition of the child's father into the household for the entire year (or for more than half the year), Lucas is now a QC for three people: Adam, Amber and the grandparents. The tiebreaker rules will apply with the option of Adam or Amber taking the QC for Lucas, each filing as single, and all related QC benefits going to one of them and none going to the other. Choosing which parent receives the benefits requires analysis of who would get the higher benefits for the child tax credit, earned income credit, exemption and dependent care credit/dependent care benefit income exclusion. Because they are unmarried, these benefits must be calculated for Adam and Amber separately. One parent can allow the other parent to claim Lucas as a QC, even if his or her AGI is higher (IRS Publication 17, supra, p. 29, Example 9). If neither parent claims the child as a QC, another tiebreaker rule allows the grandparents to claim their grandson as a QC if their AGI is higher than Adam or Amber's AGI. All the benefits are assigned to the person claiming an exemption for Lucas and cannot be divided between the three parties.

## Example 7

All the facts are the same as in Example 6, except that Adam and Amber are married.

Lucas is a QC for his parents and grandparents. If Adam and Amber file a joint return, they can claim the child as a QC and will be entitled to all of the QC benefits. If the couple files separately, they'll lose the earned income credit and dependent care credit, but one of them may claim Lucas for all remaining QC benefits. As an alternative, Lucas's parents can forgo the QC exemption and all related benefits and allow the grandparents to claim him if the grandparents' AGI is higher. To determine the higher AGI, the younger couple's AGI can be split equally on a joint return and compared to the grandparents' AGI for purposes of this test (IRS Publication 17, supra, p. 29, Example 6).

**Example 8**
All the facts are the same as in Example 6, except that Dennis, Adam's four-year-old son from another relationship, also lives in the household with Amber's parents.
Dennis meets all five QC tests as Adam's QC. Adam can claim all previously mentioned benefits for Dennis that are otherwise available. Dennis cannot be a QR for Amber or Amber's parents, (assuming Dennis is a full-year resident in the household), as he is Adam's QC. Adam and Amber are not married at year end. Lucas is a QC of Adam, Amber and his grandparents. Adam or Amber can claim Lucas as a QC for all the QC benefits otherwise available. Adam and Amber would have to file as single, since her parents are providing the household; no head of household filing status is available. The tiebreaker rules apply and will allow Adam and Amber to select which parent will claim the QC benefits for Lucas, with the other parent forgoing the benefits. The parent with the higher AGI can allow the parent with the lower AGI to claim Lucas as a QC. Adam and Amber can also allow her parents to claim Lucas as a QC if the older couple's AGI is higher. Adam and Amber would then forgo all benefits for Lucas when they allow the grandparents these benefits (IRS Publication 17, supra, p. 29, Example 9).

**Example 9**

All of the facts are the same as in Example 8, except Amber and Adam are married.

Lucas and Dennis are QC of Adam and Amber as the relationship includes stepchildren to treat Dennis as Amber's QC. Adam and Amber can claim both children as QC on a jointly filed return. Lucas is a QC of Adam and Amber and his grandparents, since Lucas lived with them for more than half of the year, meeting the residency test and the other QC tests. Where a QC is a QC of two different parties, the tiebreaker rules apply. Adam and Amber can allow her parents to claim Lucas as a QC if the older couple's AGI is higher than Adam and Amber's AGI when split equally. Amber and Adam forgo all benefits of the QC for Lucas when they allow her parents these benefits (IRS Publication 17, supra, p. 29, Example 6).

Do the tiebreaker rules apply to Dennis in the same manner as they do for Lucas, allowing Amber's parents to claim Dennis as a qualifying child? In my opinion, Adam and Amber cannot allow her parents to claim Dennis as a QC, since there is no direct, biological relationship between Dennis and Amber's parents. IRS publications never mentioned allowing a parent (Amber) to shift a stepchild exemption to grandparents who are not biologically related to the stepchild.

The relationship definition on page 25 of Publication 17, as it relates to step relatives, applies in the following manner. If Amber was a stepdaughter of her parents, than Amber's child would satisfy the QC relationship test for her step parents, as the child is a direct descendant of a stepchild. Amber's stepchild Dennis is her QC. He does not meet the QC test for her parents, as he is not a direct descendant of their daughter (the relationship test).

**Summary**

We've looked at how the QC and QR rules apply when children, parents, grandparents and unrelated individuals live together in the same household. This can sometimes be a confusing issue. Hopefully, the examples given helped clarify these rules. Tax preparers must be diligent in their fact gathering, and then carefully analyze the facts in order to provide their clients with the maximum benefits allowed for each individual situation.

## Preamble Proposed Regulations 137604–07

Withdrawal of notice of proposed rulemaking and notice of proposed rulemaking

## AGENCY:

Internal Revenue Service (IRS), Treasury.

## ACTION:

Withdrawal of notice of proposed rulemaking and notice of proposed rulemaking.

## SUMMARY:

This document withdraws proposed regulations relating to the definition of an authorized placement agency for purposes of a dependency exemption for a child placed for adoption that were issued prior to the changes made to the law by the Working Families Tax Relief Act of 2004 (WFTRA). This document contains proposed regulations that reflect changes made by WFTRA and by the Fostering Connections to Success and Increasing Adoptions Act of 2008 (FCSIAA) relating to the dependency exemption. This document also contains proposed regulations that, to reflect current law, amend the regulations relating to the surviving spouse and head of household filing statuses, the tax tables for individuals, the child and dependent care credit, the earned income credit, the standard deduction, joint tax returns, and taxpayer identification numbers for children placed for adoption. These proposed regulations change the IRS's position regarding the category of taxpayers permitted to claim the childless earned income credit. In determining a taxpayer's eligibility to claim a dependency exemption, these proposed regulations change the IRS's position regarding the adjusted gross income of a

268

taxpayer filing a joint return for purposes of the tiebreaker rules and the source of support of certain payments that originated as governmental payments. These regulations provide guidance to individuals who may claim certain child-related tax benefits.

## DATES:

Written or electronic comments and requests for a public hearing must be received by April 19, 2017.

## ADDRESSES:

Send submissions to: CC:PA:LPD:PR (REG–137604–07), Room 5203, Internal Revenue Service, PO Box 7604, Ben Franklin Station, Washington, DC 20044. Submissions may be hand-delivered Monday through Friday between the hours of 8 a.m. and 4 p.m. to CC:PA:LPD:PR (REG–137604–07), Courier's Desk, Internal Revenue Service, 1111 Constitution Avenue, NW., Washington, DC 20224, or sent electronically via the Federal eRulemaking Portal at *www.regulations.gov* (IRS REG–137604–07).

## FOR FURTHER INFORMATION CONTACT:

Concerning the proposed regulations, Victoria J. Driscoll, (202) 317-4718; concerning the submission of comments and requests for a public hearing, Regina Johnson, (202) 317-6901 (not toll-free numbers).

## SUPPLEMENTARY INFORMATION:

Background

This document withdraws a notice of proposed rulemaking (REG–107279–00) amending § 1.152–2(c)(2) of the Income

Tax Regulations that was published in the **Federal Register** (65 FR 71277) on November 30, 2000 (2000 proposed regulations) relating to the definition of an authorized placement agency for purposes of a dependency exemption for a child placed for adoption under prior law. Prior law required that a child be placed with the taxpayer for adoption by an authorized placement agency. Section 152 of the Internal Revenue Code was amended by section 201 of WFTRA (Public Law 108–311, 118 Stat. 1166, 1169) to provide that a qualifying child eligible to be the dependent of a taxpayer may include a child lawfully placed with the taxpayer for adoption. Accordingly, the proposed regulations in § 1.152–2(c)(2) under prior law are withdrawn.

This document also contains proposed amendments to 26 CFR Part 1 under sections 2, 3, 21, 32, 63, 151, 152, 6013, and to Part 301 under section 6109 to reflect the changes made by WFTRA and FCSIAA (Public Law 110–351, 122 Stat. 3949) relating to the dependency exemption, as well as changes to these sections by other acts. WFTRA amended section 152, in part, to provide a uniform definition of a qualifying child; FCSIAA added to the definition of a qualifying child the requirements that the child must be younger than the taxpayer and that the child must not file a joint return (other than as a claim for refund). FCSIAA also amended the rules that apply if two or more taxpayers are eligible to claim an individual as a qualifying child.

## 1. Dependency Rules

Under section 151, a taxpayer may deduct an exemption amount for a dependent as defined in section 152. Prior to WFTRA, section 151 contained many of the rules related to the definition of a dependent. WFTRA moved those rules to section 152. As amended, section 152(a) defines a *dependent* as a qualifying child or a qualifying relative. Taxpayers should note that a taxpayer's treatment of the dependency exemption under section 151 for a particular qualifying child or qualifying relative might have tax consequences under other Code provisions, such as the education tax credits under section 25A, the premium tax credit under section 36B, and the penalty for failure to maintain minimum essential coverage under section 5000A.

## a. Individual not a dependent

Section 152(b) provides that an individual who is a qualifying child or a qualifying relative of a taxpayer is not a taxpayer's dependent in certain circumstances. Section 152(b)(2) provides that, to be a dependent of a taxpayer, an individual must not have filed a joint return with his or her spouse. However, the WFTRA conference report provides that the "restriction does not apply if the return was filed solely to obtain a refund and no tax liability would exist for either spouse if they filed separate returns." See H.R. Rep. No. 108–696, at 55 n.38 (2004) (Conf. Rep.).

## b. Qualifying child

WFTRA established under section 152(c) a uniform definition of a qualifying child. The legislative history identifies five child-related benefits to which the uniform definition applies: the filing status of head of household under section 2(b), the child and dependent care credit under section 21, the child tax credit under section 24, the earned income credit under section 32, and the dependency exemption under section 151. See H.R. Rep. No. 108–696, at 55–65.

Section 152(c) defines a qualifying child as an individual who bears a certain relationship to the taxpayer (qualifying child relationship test), has the same principal place of abode as the taxpayer for more than one-half of the taxable year (residency test), is younger than the taxpayer and is under the age of 19 (or age 24 if a full-time student or any age if permanently and totally disabled) (age test), does not provide more than one-half of his or her own support (qualifying child support test), and does not file a joint return with a spouse except to claim a refund of estimated or withheld taxes (joint return test).

## c. Temporary absence

A child is considered to reside in the same principal place of abode as a taxpayer during a temporary absence. Under the existing section 152 regulations, a nonpermanent failure to occupy a common abode by reason of illness, education, business, vacation, military service, or a custody agreement may be a temporary absence due to special circumstances. The existing regulations under section 2 defining surviving spouse and head of household include a similar rule relating to the effect of a temporary absence on the requirement to maintain a household, but add the requirement that it is reasonable to assume that the absent person will return to the household. Under case law, a factor to consider in determining whether an absence is temporary is whether the individual intends to establish a new principal place of abode. In *Rowe v. Commissioner*, 128 T.C. 13 (2007), the court concluded that it was reasonable to assume that a taxpayer would return to her home after pretrial confinement and that the taxpayer's absence was temporary. See also *Hein v. Commissioner*, 28 T.C. 826 (1957) (*acq.*, 1958–2 CB 6), and Rev. Rul. 66–28 (1966–1 CB 31).

## d. Two or more taxpayers eligible to claim individual as qualifying child

Section 152(c)(4) provides tiebreaker rules that apply if an individual meets the definition of a qualifying child for two or more taxpayers (eligible taxpayers). In general, the eligible taxpayer who is a parent (eligible parent) of the individual may claim the individual as a qualifying child or, if there is no eligible parent, then the individual may be claimed by the eligible taxpayer with the highest adjusted gross income.

If more than one of the eligible taxpayers is a parent of the individual, more than one eligible parent claims the individual as a qualifying child, and the eligible parents claiming the individual do not file a joint return with each other, the individual is treated as the qualifying child of the eligible parent claiming the individual with whom the individual resided for the longest period of time during the taxable year. If the individual resided with each eligible parent claiming the individual for the same amount of time during the taxable year, the individual is treated as the qualifying child of the eligible parent claiming the individual with the highest adjusted gross income.

If at least one, but not all, of two or more eligible taxpayers is a parent of the individual, but no eligible parent claims the individual as a qualifying child, another eligible taxpayer may claim the individual, but only if the eligible taxpayer's adjusted gross income is higher than the adjusted gross income of each eligible parent. Since 2009, IRS Publication 501, *Exemptions, Standard Deduction, and Filing Information*, has stated that "[i]f the child's parents file a joint return with each other, this rule may be applied by dividing the parents' combined AGI equally between the parents."

Notice 2006–86 (2006–2 CB 680) provides interim guidance on these rules prior to the amendments by FCSIAA. The notice provides that, except to the extent that a noncustodial parent may claim the child as a qualifying child under the special rule for divorced or separated parents in section 152(e), discussed in the next paragraph, if more than one taxpayer claims a child as a qualifying child, the child is treated as the qualifying child of only one taxpayer (as determined under the tiebreaker rules of section 152(c)(4)) for purposes of the five provisions subject to the uniform definition of a qualifying child (the filing status of head of household under section 2(b), the child and dependent care credit under section 21, the child tax credit under section 24, the earned income credit under section 32, and the dependency exemption under section 151, as well as for purposes of the exclusion for dependent care assistance under section 129 (which may apply to the care of a dependent qualifying child under age 13)). Thus, in general, the tiebreaker rules for determining which taxpayer may claim a child as a qualifying child apply to these provisions as a group, rather than on a section-by-section basis.

Notice 2006–86 contains an exception to the rule that only one taxpayer may claim a child as a qualifying child for all purposes. Section 152(e) has a special rule for divorced or separated parents that determines who, as between the custodial and noncustodial parent, may claim a child as a qualifying child or qualifying relative if certain tests (different from the general tests under sections 152(c) and (d)) regarding residency and support are met and the custodial parent releases a claim to exemption for the child. The notice provides that, if this special rule applies, a noncustodial parent may claim a child as a qualifying child for purposes of the dependency exemption and the child tax credit (the only two of the provisions addressed in the notice to which section 152(e) applies in determining who is a qualifying child), and another taxpayer may claim the child for one or more of the other benefits to which section 152(e) does not apply.

Although FCSIAA affects other aspects of section 152(c)(4) and Notice 2006–86, there is nothing in FCSIAA that would compel a change in the rule described in Notice 2006–86 that an individual is treated as the qualifying child of only one taxpayer for the listed child-related tax benefits, except if the special rule in section 152(e) applies.

## e. Qualifying relative

Under section 152(d), a qualifying relative is an individual who bears a certain relationship to the taxpayer, including an individual who has the same principal place of abode as the taxpayer and is a member of the taxpayer's household for the taxable year (qualifying relative relationship test), has gross income less than the exemption amount for the taxable year (gross income test), receives more than one-half of his or her support from the taxpayer (qualifying relative support test), and is not a qualifying child of any taxpayer (not a qualifying child test).

Notice 2008–5 (2008–1 CB 256) addresses whether a taxpayer meets the test under section 152(d)(1)(D) to claim an individual as a qualifying relative. That provision requires that the individual not be a qualifying child of either the taxpayer or any other taxpayer during a taxable year beginning in the calendar year in which the taxpayer's taxable year begins. The notice provides that, for purposes of section 152(d)(1)(D), an individual is not a qualifying child of "any other taxpayer" if the individual's parent (or other person for whom the individual is defined as a qualifying child) is not required by section 6012 to file an income tax return and (1) does not file an income tax return, or (2) files an income tax return solely to obtain a refund of withheld income taxes.

## f. Support tests

Under section 152(c)(1)(D), to be a taxpayer's qualifying child, an individual must not have provided over one-half of the individual's own support for the calendar year. Under section 152(d)(1)(C), to be a taxpayer's qualifying relative, a taxpayer must have provided over one-half of an individual's support for the calendar year.

Regarding governmental payments to a person with a qualifying need, the WFTRA conference report, H.R. Rep. No. 108–696, at 57, states that "[g]overnmental payments and subsidies (e.g., Temporary Assistance [for] Needy Families, food stamps, and housing) generally are treated as support provided by a third party." The IRS has successfully asserted in litigation that governmental payments provided to a parent to aid a family with dependent children and used by the parent for support of her children was support of the children provided by the government, and not support provided by the parent. See *Lutter v. Commissioner*, 61 T.C. 685 (1974), *affd. per curiam*, 514 F.2d 1095 (7th Cir. 1975).

## 2. Surviving Spouse and Head of Household, and Conforming Changes

Prior to amendment by section 803(b) of the Tax Reform Act of 1969 (Public Law 91–172, 83 Stat. 487), section 2(a) provided that the return of a surviving spouse is treated as a joint return for purposes of the tax rates, the tax tables for individuals, and the standard deduction. Following the 1969 amendments, section 2(a) defines the term *surviving spouse* for purposes of section 1. The return of a taxpayer filing as a surviving spouse is no longer treated as a joint return under sections 2, 3, or 63. Section 3 provides tax tables for certain individuals in lieu of the tax imposed by section 1. Section 63(c) provides the same basic standard deduction for a taxpayer filing as a surviving spouse as a taxpayer filing a joint return. Accordingly, a taxpayer filing as a surviving spouse is no longer treated as filing a joint return for any tax purpose, but rather, a taxpayer filing as a surviving spouse simply uses the same tax rates under section 1, the same amounts in the tax tables under section 3, and the same standard deduction under section 63 as a taxpayer filing a joint return.

Generally, under section 2(b), to qualify as a head of household, a taxpayer must maintain a household that is the principal place of abode of a qualifying child or other dependent for more than one-half of the taxable year. If the dependent is a parent of the taxpayer and the parent does not share a principal place of abode with the taxpayer, the household maintained by the taxpayer must be the parent's principal place of abode for the entire taxable year.

Prior to WFTRA, section 21 required that a taxpayer maintain a household to claim the credit for dependent care expenses, and regulations on maintaining a household were published under that section. WFTRA removed that requirement from the dependent care credit.

## 3. Earned Income Credit

Section 32 provides a tax credit to eligible taxpayers who work and have earned income below a certain dollar amount. Before the amendment of section 32 by the Omnibus Reconciliation Act of 1993 (Public Law 103–66, 107 Stat. 312), the earned income credit (EIC) was allowable only to a taxpayer with one or more qualifying children. If an individual met the definition of a qualifying child for more than one taxpayer, a tiebreaker rule in section 32 determined which taxpayer was allowed to claim the individual as a qualifying child for the EIC. For taxable years beginning after 1993, section 32(c)(1)(A)(ii) allows a taxpayer without a qualifying child to claim the EIC (childless EIC) if certain requirements are met. Although there is no regulatory guidance on this issue, since 1995, the IRS has taken the position in IRS Publication 596, *Earned Income Credit*, that if an individual meets the definition of a qualifying child for more than one taxpayer and the individual is not treated as the qualifying child of a taxpayer under the tiebreaker rules, then that taxpayer is precluded from claiming the childless EIC. WFTRA moved the tiebreaker rules from section 32 to section 152(c)(4).

277

Before repeal in 2010, section 3507 allowed advance payment of the EIC. Section 3507 was repealed by the FAA Air Transportation Modernization and Safety Improvement Act (Public Law 111–226, 124 Stat. 2389).

### 4. Additional Standard Deduction for the Aged and Blind

Before the amendments to sections 63 and 151 made by the Tax Reform Act of 1986 (Public Law 99–514, 100 Stat. 2085), a taxpayer was entitled to an additional personal exemption under section 151 for the taxpayer or the taxpayer's spouse (or both), if either was age 65 or older or was blind at the close of the taxable year. As amended, section 63 provides an additional standard deduction for age or blindness instead of an additional personal exemption under section 151.

### Proposed Regulations Explanation

The proposed regulations reflect statutory amendments to sections 2, 3, 21, 32, 63, 151, 152, 6013, and 6109. In addition, the regulations address certain significant issues arising under these sections and modify certain IRS positions, as explained below.

### 1. Dependency Exemption

Consistent with the amendments made to sections 151 and 152 by WFTRA, the proposed regulations move rules related to the definition of a dependent from the regulations under section 151 to the regulations under section 152.

### a. Relationship test

### i. General Rules

Section 152(c)(2) provides that a qualifying child must be a child or a descendant of a child of the taxpayer, or a brother, sister, stepbrother, or stepsister of the taxpayer, or a descendant of any of these relatives. Section 152(d)(2) provides that a qualifying relative must bear a certain relationship to the taxpayer, which includes a child or a descendant of a child, a brother, sister, stepbrother, stepsister, parent or ancestor of a parent, or an aunt or uncle of the taxpayer. An individual (other than the taxpayer's spouse) who is not related to the taxpayer in one of the named relationships nevertheless may satisfy the relationship test for a qualifying relative if the individual has the same principal place of abode as the taxpayer and is a member of the taxpayer's household for the taxpayer's taxable year.

The proposed regulations adopt the rule in Notice 2008–5 regarding whether an individual is a qualifying child of a taxpayer for purposes of determining whether that individual may be a qualifying relative. That is, the proposed regulations provide that an individual is not a qualifying child of a person if that person is not required to file an income tax return under section 6012, and either does not file an income tax return or files an income tax return solely to claim a refund of estimated or withheld taxes.

## ii. Adopted Child—Adoption by Individual Other than the Taxpayer

Prior to 2005, for purposes of the relationship test, a person's legally adopted child was treated as that person's child by blood. Specifically, section 152(b)(2) provided that "a legally adopted child of an individual (and a child who is a member of an individual's household, if placed with such individual by an authorized placement agency for legal adoption by such individual), . . . shall be treated as a child of such individual by blood." Therefore, a taxpayer other than the adopting "individual" could be eligible to claim an exemption for an adopted child. For example, the parent of the adopting parent could claim a dependency exemption for the legally adopted child of the taxpayer's son or daughter (just as biological grandparents may claim an exemption for a grandchild) if all other requirements were met.

WFTRA amended section 152 to change the reference from a child placed by an authorized placement agency for adoption to a child who is "lawfully placed" for legal adoption. In making that change, however, WFTRA also changed the reference to the adopting person from "an individual" to "the taxpayer," so that section 152(f)(1)(B) currently provides that a legally adopted individual of the taxpayer is treated as a child by blood of the taxpayer. The use of the word "taxpayer" rather than "individual" arguably limits the recognition of a relationship through adoption only to those situations in which the taxpayer claiming a dependency exemption for the child is the person who adopts the child. This interpretation of the amended statutory language would diverge from the results of a legal adoption under property, inheritance, and other nontax law, and from the prior tax treatment of adoptions – a significant change in the applicable law. However, there is nothing in the legislative history indicating that Congress intended to limit the treatment of an adopted child as a child by blood in this manner or that otherwise suggests this change in language was intended to effect a change in existing law.

To fill this apparent gap in the statute, the proposed regulations provide that any child legally adopted by a "person," or any child who is placed with a "person" for legal adoption by that "person," is treated as a child by blood of that person for purposes of the relationship tests under sections 152(c)(2) and 152(d)(2). Similarly, the proposed regulations provide that an eligible foster child is a child who is placed with a "person" rather than with a taxpayer.

### iii. Adopted Child and Foster Child—Child Placement

Although WFTRA removed the reference to an authorized placement agency from the provisions relating to an adopted child in section 152(f)(1)(B), the reference to an authorized placement agency continues to appear in section 152(f)(1)(C), relating to an eligible foster child. Prior to amendment by WFTRA, section 152 treated a child who was a member of an individual's household pending adoption as a child by blood of the individual for purposes of the relationship test only if the child was a foster child living with the individual or if the child was placed with the individual by an authorized placement agency for adoption by the individual. Similarly, § 301.6109–3(a) currently provides that a taxpayer may obtain an adoption taxpayer identification number (ATIN) only for a child who was placed for adoption by an authorized placement agency.

As amended by WFTRA, section 152 treats a child placed for adoption as a child by blood of the taxpayer if the child "is lawfully placed with the taxpayer for legal adoption by the taxpayer." A child may be lawfully placed for legal adoption by an authorized placement agency, the child's parents, or other persons authorized by State law to place children for legal adoption. These proposed regulations reflect the changes made by WFTRA and amend the regulations under section 6109 to provide that the IRS will assign an ATIN to a child who has been lawfully placed with a person for legal adoption.

Under section 152(f)(1)(A)(ii) and § 1.152–1(b)(1)(iii) of these proposed regulations, the term *child* also includes an eligible foster child of the taxpayer as defined in 152(f)(1)(C), that is, a child who is placed with the taxpayer by an authorized placement agency or by the judgment, decree, or other order of a court of competent jurisdiction.

### iv. Definition of Authorized Placement Agency

The 2000 proposed regulations under § 1.152–2(c)(2) defined an authorized placement agency for purposes of the prior law regarding a child placed for legal adoption. These proposed regulations define an authorized placement agency for purposes of the definition of an eligible foster child and withdraw the 2000 proposed regulations, which defined that term without reference to an Indian Tribal Government (ITG).

These proposed regulations provide that an *authorized placement agency* may be a State, the District of Columbia, a possession of the United States, a foreign country, an agency or organization authorized by, or a political subdivision of, any of these entities to place children in foster care or for adoption. Under the Indian Child Welfare Act of 1978 (25 U.S.C. chapter 21), ITGs and states perform similar functions for foster care and adoption programs. Thus, the proposed regulations provide that an authorized placement agency also may be an ITG (as defined in section 7701(a)(40)), or an agency or organization authorized by, or a political subdivision of, an ITG that places children in foster care or for adoption.

### b. *Residency test—principal place of abode*

For purposes of determining whether an individual has the same principal place of abode as the taxpayer in applying the residency test for a qualifying child and the relationship test for a qualifying relative who does not have one of the listed relationships to the taxpayer, the proposed regulations provide that the term *principal place of abode* means a person's main home or dwelling where the person resides. A person's principal place of abode need not be the same physical location throughout the taxable year and may be temporary lodging such as a homeless shelter or relief housing resulting from displacement caused by a natural disaster.

The proposed regulations further provide that a taxpayer and an individual have the same principal place of abode despite a temporary absence by either person. A person is temporarily absent if, based on the facts and circumstances, the person would have resided with the taxpayer but for the temporary absence and it is reasonable to assume the person will return to reside at the place of abode. Thus, the proposed regulations adopt the "reasonable to assume" language from the existing regulations under section 2. The proposed regulations indicate that a nonpermanent failure to occupy the abode by reason of illness, education, business, vacation, military service, institutionalized care for a child who is permanently and totally disabled (as defined in section 22(e)(3)), or incarceration may be treated as a temporary absence due to special circumstances. This definition of temporary absence applies to the residency test for a qualifying child, to the relationship test for a qualifying relative who does not have a listed relationship to the taxpayer, and to the requirements to maintain a household for surviving spouse and head of household.

For purposes of the residency test for a qualifying child, the proposed regulations provide that an individual is treated as having the same principal place of abode as the taxpayer for more than one-half of the taxable year if the individual resides with the taxpayer for at least 183 nights during the taxpayer's taxable year or for at least 184 nights during the taxpayer's taxable year that includes a leap day (residing for more than one-half of the taxable year). The proposed regulations further provide that an individual resides with the taxpayer for a night if the individual sleeps (1) at the taxpayer's residence, or (2) in the company of the taxpayer when the individual does not sleep at the taxpayer's residence (for example, when the parent and the child are on vacation). The regulations provide additional rules for counting nights if a night extends over two taxable years and for taxpayers who work at night.

The proposed regulations provide special rules for determining whether an individual satisfies a residency test if the individual is born or dies during the taxable year, is adopted or placed for adoption, is an eligible foster child, or is a missing child.

### c. *Age test*

The age test for a qualifying child requires that an individual be younger than the taxpayer claiming the individual as a qualifying child, and the individual must not have attained the age of 19 (or age 24 if the individual is a student). The age requirement is treated as satisfied if the individual is permanently and totally disabled.

For purposes of this age test, the proposed regulations substantially adopt the existing definition of a student. Accordingly, the proposed regulations provide that the term *student* means an individual who, during some part of each of 5 calendar months during the calendar year in which the taxable year of the taxpayer begins, is a full-time student at an educational organization described in section 170(b)(1)(A)(ii) or is pursuing a full-time course of institutional on-farm training under the supervision of an accredited agent of an educational institution or of a State or political subdivision of a State. An *educational organization*, as defined in section 170(b)(1)(A)(ii), is a school normally maintaining a regular faculty and curriculum and having a regularly enrolled body of students in attendance at the place where its educational activities are regularly carried on.

### d. *Support tests*

In determining whether an individual provided more than one-half of the individual's own support (qualifying child support test), or whether a taxpayer provided more than one-half of an individual's support (qualifying relative support test), the proposed regulations compare the amount of support provided by the individual or the taxpayer to the total amount of the individual's support from all sources. In general, the amount of an individual's support from all sources includes support the individual provides and income that is excludable from gross income. The proposed regulations further provide that the amount of an item of support is the amount of expenses paid or incurred to furnish the item of support. If support is furnished in the form of property or a benefit (such as lodging), the amount of that support is the fair market value of the item furnished (Rev. Rul. 58–302 (1958–1 CB 62)).

The proposed regulations provide that the term *support* includes food, shelter, clothing, medical and dental care, education, and similar items for the benefit of the supported individual. Support does not include Federal, State, and local income taxes, or Social Security and Medicare taxes, of an individual paid from the individual's own income (Rev. Rul. 58–67 (1958–1 CB 62)), funeral expenses (Rev. Rul. 65–307 (1965–2 CB 40)), life insurance premiums, or scholarships received by a taxpayer's child who is a student as defined in section 152(f)(2).

The proposed regulations provide that medical insurance premiums are treated as support. These premiums include Part A Basic Medicare premiums, if any, under Title XVIII of the Social Security Act (42 U.S.C. 1395c to 1395i–5), Part B Supplemental Medicare premiums under Title XVIII of the Social Security Act (42 U.S.C. 1395j to 1395w–6), Part C Medicare + Choice Program premiums under Title XVIII of the Social Security Act (42 U.S.C. 1395w–21 to 1395w–29), and Part D Voluntary Prescription Drug Benefit Medicare premiums under Title XVIII of the Social Security Act (42 U.S.C. 1395w–101 to 1395w–154). However, medical insurance proceeds, including benefits received under Medicare Part A, Part B, Part C, and Part D, are not treated as support and are disregarded in determining the amount of the individual's support. Thus, only the premiums paid and the unreimbursed portion of the expenses for the individual's medical care are support. See Rev. Rul. 64–223 (1964–2 CB 50); and Rev. Rul. 70–341 (1970–2 CB 31), revoked in part by Rev. Rul. 79–173 (1979–1 CB 86) to the extent that it held that Part A Medicare benefits are included as a recipient's contribution to support. In addition, services provided to individuals under the medical and dental care provisions of the Armed Forces Act (10 U.S.C. chapter 55) are not treated as support and are disregarded in determining the amount of the individual's support. Finally, payments from a third party (including a third party's insurance company) for the medical care of an injured individual in satisfaction of a legal claim for the personal injury of the individual are not items of support and are disregarded in determining the amount of the individual's support. See Rev. Rul. 64–223.

The proposed regulations provide that, in general, governmental payments and subsidies are treated as support provided by a third party. Consistent with previously issued rulings and case law, these payments and subsidies include, for example, Temporary Assistance for Needy Families (TANF) (42 U.S.C. 601–619), low-income housing assistance (42 U.S.C. 1437f), benefits under the Supplemental Nutrition Assistance Program (7 U.S.C. chapter 51), Supplemental Security Income payments (42 U.S.C. 1381–1383f), foster care maintenance payments, and adoption assistance payments. See H.R. Rep. No. 108–696, at 57 (2004) (Conf. Rep.); *Gulvin v. Commissioner*, 644 F.2d 2 (5th Cir. 1981); and Rev. Rul. 74–153 (1974–1 CB 20).

However, unlike the subsidies described in the previous paragraph that generally are based solely on need, old age benefits under section 202(b) of Title II of the Social Security Act (SSA) (42 U.S.C. 402) are based on an individual's earnings and contributions into the Social Security system and thus are treated as support provided by the recipient to the extent the recipient uses the payments for support. See Rev.

Rul. 58–419 (1958–2 CB 57), as modified by Rev. Rul. 64–222 (1964–2 CB 47). Similarly, Social Security survivor and disability insurance benefit payments made under section 202(d) of the SSA to the child of a deceased or disabled parent are treated as support provided by the child to the extent those payments are used for the child's support. See Rev. Rul. 57–344 (1957–2 CB 112) and Rev. Rul. 74–543 (1974–2 CB 39).

The proposed regulations provide a special rule for governmental payments used by the recipient or other intended beneficiary to support another individual. The proposed regulations draw a distinction between: (1) governmental payments (such as Social Security old age benefits, or survivor and disability insurance benefits for a child) made to a recipient that are intended to benefit a particular named individual (whether the recipient, or another intended beneficiary for whom the recipient merely acts as the payee on behalf of that other intended beneficiary); and (2) governmental payments made to a recipient that are intended to support the recipient and other individuals (such as TANF). Although the governmental payments of the former variety are intended to benefit a particular named individual, because money is fungible, the intended beneficiary might use the governmental payments to support another individual. In this situation, the proposed regulations provide that, if the intended beneficiary (whether the recipient or another individual) uses the governmental payments to support another individual, that amount would constitute support of that other individual provided by the intended beneficiary. Similarly, the proposed regulations provide that the use of governmental payments of the latter variety by the recipient to support another individual would constitute support of that other individual provided by the recipient, whereas any part of such a payment used for the support of the recipient would constitute support of the recipient by a third party. For example, if a mother receives TANF and uses the TANF payments to support her children, the proposed regulations treat the mother as having provided that support. Thus, the IRS will no longer assert the position that it took in *Lutter*, which concerned payments received by a mother under a program that was the predecessor of TANF. The Treasury Department and the IRS are proposing this rule for the administrative convenience of both the IRS and taxpayers to avoid the need to trace the use of such governmental payments, as opposed to the use of other funds of the recipient, for the support of another individual.

The Treasury Department and IRS request comments on whether various payments made pursuant to the Patient Protection And Affordable Care Act (Public Law 111–148, 124 Stat. 119) in the form of a cost-sharing reduction, an advanced payment of the premium tax credit, or as a reimbursement of health insurance premiums in the form of a premium tax credit, when used for the benefit of another individual, are support provided by the recipient of those benefits or support provided by a third party.

### e. *Citizenship*

Under section 152(b)(3)(A), an individual who is not a citizen or national of the United States is not a dependent unless the individual is a resident of the United States, Canada, or Mexico. Nevertheless, consistent with the exception for certain adopted children in section 152(b)(3)(B), the proposed regulations provide that an adopted child of a taxpayer who is a U.S. citizen or national may qualify as a dependent if, for the taxpayer's taxable year, the child has the same principal place of abode as the taxpayer and is a member of the taxpayer's household, and otherwise qualifies as the taxpayer's dependent.

### f. *Tiebreaker rules*

The proposed regulations change the interpretation in Publication 501 regarding a taxpayer's adjusted gross income on a joint return and provide that, in applying the tiebreaker rules that treat an individual as the qualifying child of the eligible taxpayer with the higher or highest adjusted gross income, the adjusted gross income of a taxpayer who files a joint tax return is the total adjusted gross income shown on the return. The prior interpretation is changed to be consistent with other Code sections that require the filing of a joint return to claim a benefit and therefore calculate income based on the entire amount shown on the joint return. For example, the earned income credit under section 32 calculates the earned income amount based on the entire amount shown on the joint return. This joint return rule also is relevant for determining whether section 152(c)(4)(C) applies. Under that provision, if an eligible parent does not claim an individual as a qualifying child, another eligible taxpayer may claim the individual as a qualifying child only if that taxpayer's adjusted gross income is higher than the adjusted gross income of any eligible parent.

The proposed regulations also expand the tiebreaker rule in section 152(c)(4)(C) to address the situation in which an eligible parent does not claim an individual as a qualifying child and two or more taxpayers, none of whom is a parent, are eligible to claim the individual as a qualifying child and each has adjusted gross income higher than any eligible parent. In this situation, the proposed regulations provide that the individual is treated as the qualifying child of the eligible taxpayer with the highest adjusted gross income.

### g. *Child of parents who are divorced, separated, or living apart*

Section 152(e) provides, in general, that a child is treated as the qualifying child or qualifying relative of a noncustodial parent for a calendar year if, among other things, the custodial parent provides to the noncustodial parent a written declaration that the custodial parent will not claim the child as a dependent for any taxable year beginning in that calendar year. Under section 152(e)(2)(B), the noncustodial parent must attach the written declaration to his or her return.

The proposed regulations provide that the noncustodial parent must attach a copy of the written declaration to an original or amended return. A taxpayer may submit a copy of the written declaration to the IRS during an examination of that parent's return. However, to provide certainty for both taxpayers and the IRS, the proposed regulations provide that a copy of a written declaration attached to an amended return or provided during an examination will not meet the requirements of section 152(e) and § 1.152–5(e) if the custodial parent signed the written declaration after the custodial parent filed a return claiming a dependency exemption for the child for the year at issue, and the custodial parent has not filed an amended return to remove that claim to a dependency exemption. The proposed regulations provide similar rules for a parent revoking a written declaration.

### h. *Filing a return solely to obtain a refund of taxes*

Individuals who file an income tax return solely to obtain a refund of estimated or withheld taxes are subject to special rules under various provisions of section 152. Section 152(c)(1)(E) provides that, for an individual to be a qualifying child of a taxpayer, the individual cannot have filed a joint return "other than only for a claim of refund." Section 152(b)(2) provides that, for an individual to be a dependent of a taxpayer, the individual cannot have filed a joint return with the individual's spouse. However, the WFTRA conference report states that "[t]his restriction does not apply if the return was filed solely to obtain a refund and no tax liability would exist for either spouse if they filed separate returns." Section 152(d)(1)(D) provides that, to be a qualifying relative, an individual may not be the qualifying child of the taxpayer or of any other taxpayer. Notice 2008–5 concludes that an individual is not the qualifying child of "any other taxpayer," within the meaning of section 152(d)(1)(D), if the person who could have claimed the individual as a qualifying child does not have a filing obligation and either does not file a return or files a return solely to obtain a refund of withheld taxes.

The proposed regulations provide a similar exception to the rule in section 152(b)(1) that a taxpayer cannot have a dependent if the taxpayer himself or herself is a dependent of another taxpayer. Specifically, the proposed regulations provide that an individual is not a dependent of a person if that person is not required to file an income tax return under section 6012 and either does not file an income tax return or files an income tax return solely to claim a refund of estimated or withheld taxes.

## 2. *Surviving Spouse, Head of Household, and Conforming Changes*

The proposed regulations amend the regulations under section 2 regarding the definition of surviving spouse and the definition of head of household to conform to the amendments made by WFTRA. To reflect the amendments made by the Tax Reform Act of 1969, the proposed regulations remove from the regulations under sections 2, 3, and 6013 references to the return of a surviving spouse being treated as a joint return. The proposed regulations also revise and move from the regulations under section 21 to the regulations under section 2 the definition of maintaining a household, in part, to conform to the amendments to section 21 made by WFTRA, which removed the requirement that a taxpayer maintain a household to claim the credit under section 21.

### a. *Surviving spouse*

From the time of the 1969 amendment until the enactment of WFTRA, section 2(a)(1)(B) provided that a taxpayer who is a surviving spouse described in section 2(a)(1)(A) may file as a

291

surviving spouse (and thus may use the tax rates of joint filers) only if the taxpayer "maintains as his home a household which constitutes for the taxable year the principal place of abode (as a member of such household) of a dependent (i) who (within the meaning of section 152) is a son, stepson, daughter, or stepdaughter of the taxpayer, and (ii) with respect to whom the taxpayer is entitled to a deduction for the taxable year under section 151." Thus, the member of the taxpayer's household had to be a son or daughter or stepson or stepdaughter for whom the taxpayer was entitled to a dependency deduction.

WFTRA amended section 2(a), as well as certain other sections such as section 42 relating to the low-income housing credit and section 125 relating to cafeteria plans, to provide that the reference to section 152 applies "without regard to subsections (b)(1), (b)(2), and (d)(1)(B)." These three subsections, respectively: (1) deny a dependency exemption to a dependent, (2) deny a dependency exemption for a person filing a joint return with his or her spouse, and (3) require the gross income of a qualifying relative to be less than the amount of the dependency exemption. Thus, the language inserted by the WFTRA technical amendment to section 2(a) was intended to broaden the class of individuals whose members could qualify a taxpayer as a surviving spouse for purposes of section 2. See also Staff of Joint Comm. on Taxation, 108th Cong., *General Explanation of Tax Legislation Enacted in the 108th Congress* 130 (Comm. Print 2005) ("technical and conforming amendments ... provide that an individual may qualify as a dependent for certain purposes ... without regard to whether the individual has gross income ... or is married and files a joint return.")

However, in amending section 2(a) for this purpose, WFTRA inserted the direction to exclude the three referenced provisions after the reference to section 152 in section 2(a)(1)(B)(i). Thus, this section currently provides, "(i) who (within the meaning of section 152, determined without regard to subsections (b)(1), (b)(2), and (d)(1)(B) thereof) is a son, stepson, daughter, or stepdaughter of the taxpayer." Because section 2(a)(1)(B)(ii) continues to require that the taxpayer be entitled to a deduction under section 151 for the dependent (a requirement that could not be met if any of these three sections applied), read literally, section 2(a)(1)(B)(ii) would override the intent of the statutory change in section 2(a)(1)(B)(i), thus preventing the WFTRA amendment from effecting any change in the statute. Therefore, to give effect to the statutory amendment, the proposed regulations construe the language added by WFTRA instead to modify the section 152 requirements that apply in determining whether the taxpayer is entitled to the dependency exemption under section 151 for purposes of section 2(a)(1)(B)(ii). Accordingly, the proposed regulations provide that an individual is a dependent for purposes of section 2(a) if the taxpayer may claim a deduction under section 151 for the individual without applying sections 152(b)(1), (b)(2), and (d)(1)(B).

### b. *Head of household*

The proposed regulations under section 2(b) update and simplify the existing regulations defining head of household. Consistent with the statutory amendments to the definition of a dependent, the proposed regulations provide rules on qualifying as a head of household by maintaining a household that is the principal place of abode of a qualifying child or a dependent. The proposed regulations on head of household apply the rules in the proposed regulations under section 152 for determining principal place of abode, including whether an absence is temporary.

### c. *Maintaining a household*

The proposed regulations provide that a taxpayer maintains a household only if the taxpayer pays more than one-half of the cost related to operating the household for the relevant period.

Expenses related to operating the household include property taxes, mortgage interest, rent, utility charges, upkeep and repairs, property insurance, and food consumed on the premises. A taxpayer may treat a home's fair market rental value as a cost of maintaining a household (instead of the sum of payments for mortgage interest, property taxes, and insurance). The proposed regulations provide rules that, in certain circumstances, prorate on a monthly basis the annual cost of maintaining a household when a qualifying child or dependent resides in the household for less than the entire taxable year. The proposed regulations also, in certain circumstances, recognize the creation of a new household during a year and treat shared living quarters as separate households.

### 3. *Tax Tables for Individuals*

The proposed regulations remove from the regulations under section 3 references to the return of a surviving spouse being treated as a joint return to conform to the amendments made by the Tax Reform Act of 1969. The proposed regulations also update the regulations under section 3 to reflect current law.

### 4. Earned Income Credit

The proposed regulations conform the regulations under section 32 to amendments made to section 32 by WFTRA. Consistent with the 2010 repeal of section 3507 by the FAA Air Transportation Modernization and Safety Improvement Act, the proposed regulations delete the paragraphs of the regulations under section 32 discussing advance payment of the earned income credit.

In addition, the proposed regulations reflect a change in the IRS's position on the interaction of sections 152(c)(4) and 32. Specifically, the proposed regulations provide that, if an individual meets the definition of a qualifying child under section 152(c)(1) for more than one taxpayer and the individual is not treated as the qualifying child of one such taxpayer under the tiebreaker rules of section 152(c)(4), then the individual also is not treated as a qualifying child of that taxpayer for purposes of section 32(c)(1)(A). Thus, that taxpayer may be an eligible individual under section 32(c)(1)(A)(ii) and may claim the childless EIC if he or she meets the other requirements of that section. The Treasury Department and the IRS have concluded that this change in position is consistent with the language and purpose of section 32 and will be less confusing to taxpayers and easier for the IRS to administer.

The problems with the current rule may be illustrated by the following example. Two sisters (B and C) live together and each of them is a low-income taxpayer. Neither has a child and each may claim the childless EIC under section 32(c)(1)(A)(ii). Later, B has a child, and B's child meets the definition of a qualifying child under section 152(c)(1) for both B and C. The child is treated as the qualifying child of B under the tiebreaker rules of section 152(c)(4), and B may claim the EIC as an eligible individual with a qualifying child under section 32(c)(1)(A)(i). Under the current rule, C would not be allowed to claim the childless EIC under section 32(c)(1)(A)(ii). The Treasury Department and the IRS have determined that allowing C to continue to claim the childless EIC after the child is born is equitable and consistent with the purpose of section 32 to assist working, low-income taxpayers. Accordingly, the proposed regulations provide that, if an individual is not treated as a qualifying child of a taxpayer after applying the tiebreaker rules of section 152(c)(4), then the individual will not prevent that taxpayer from qualifying for the childless EIC.

## 5. *Additional Standard Deduction for the Aged and Blind*

The proposed regulations remove the provisions on additional exemptions for age and blindness from the regulations under section 151 and add regulations under section 63 on the additional standard deduction for the aged and the blind to reflect the changes made by the Tax Reform Act of 1986. The proposed regulations amend the regulations under section 63 to remove a cross reference to now-repealed statutory provisions relating to a charitable deduction for taxpayers who do not itemize. To limit impediments to electronic filing, the proposed regulations also delete the requirement that a taxpayer claiming a tax benefit for blindness must attach a certificate or statement to the taxpayer's tax return. Instead, a taxpayer must maintain the certificate or statement in the taxpayer's records.

## Applicability Date

These regulations are proposed to apply to taxable years beginning after the date the regulations are published as final regulations in the **Federal Register**. Pending the issuance of the final regulations, taxpayers may choose to apply these proposed regulations in any open taxable years.

## Effect on Other Documents

When finalized, the proposed regulations will obsolete Rev. Rul. 57–344, Rev. Rul. 58–67, Rev. Rul. 58–302, Rev. Rul. 64–223, Rev. Rul. 65–307, Rev. Rul. 70–341, Rev. Rul. 74–153, Rev. Rul. 74–543, Rev. Rul. 79–173, Rev. Rul. 84–89, Notice 2006–86, and Notice 2008–5.

## Special Analyses

Certain IRS regulations, including these, are exempt from the requirements of Executive Order 12866, as supplemented and reaffirmed by Executive Order 13563. Therefore, a regulatory impact assessment is not required. The regulations affect individuals and do not impose a collection of information on small entities, therefore the Regulatory Flexibility Act (5 U.S.C. chapter 6) does not apply. Pursuant to section 7805(f) of the Code, this notice of proposed rulemaking will be submitted to the Chief Counsel for Advocacy of the Small Business Administration for comment on its impact on small business.

## Statement of Availability of IRS Documents

IRS revenue procedures, revenue rulings, notices and other guidance cited in this preamble are published in the Internal Revenue Bulletin (or Cumulative Bulletin) and are available from the Superintendent of Documents, U.S. Government Publishing Office, Washington, DC 20402, or by visiting the IRS website at http://www.irs.gov.

## Comments and Requests for a Public Hearing

Before these proposed regulations are adopted as final regulations, consideration will be given to any comments that are submitted timely to the IRS, as prescribed in this preamble under the "Addresses" heading. The IRS and Treasury Department request comments on all aspects of the proposed rules. All comments will be available at www.regulations.gov or upon request. A public hearing will be scheduled if requested in writing by any person that timely submits written comments. If a public hearing is scheduled, notice of the date, time, and place for the hearing will be published in the **Federal Register**.

### Drafting Information

The principal authors of these proposed regulations are Christina M. Glendening and Victoria J. Driscoll of the Office of Associate Chief Counsel (Income Tax and Accounting). However, other personnel from the Treasury Department and the IRS participated in the development of the regulations.

## Withdrawal of Notice of Proposed Rulemaking

Accordingly, under authority of 26 U.S.C. 7805, the notice of proposed rulemaking (REG–107279–00) that was published in the **Federal Register** on November 30, 2000 (65 FR 71277), is withdrawn.

End of Preamble

### Proposed Amendments to the Regulations

Accordingly, 26 CFR Parts 1 and 301 are proposed to be amended as follows:

### PART 1—INCOME TAXES

Paragraph 1. The authority citation for part 1 continues to read, in part, as follows:

Authority: 26 U.S.C. 7805 * * *

Par. 2. Section 1.2–1 is revised to read as follows:

### § 1.2–1 Returns of surviving spouse and head of household.

(a) *In general*. Tax is determined under section 1(a) for a return of a surviving spouse, as defined in section 2(a) and § 1.2–2(a). Tax is determined under section 1(b) for a return of a head of household, as defined in section 2(b) and § 1.2–2(b).

(b) *Death of a spouse.* If married taxpayers have different taxable years solely because of the death of either spouse, the taxable year of the deceased spouse is deemed to end on the last day of the surviving spouse's taxable year for purposes of determining their eligibility to file a joint return for that year. For rules relating to filing a joint return in the year a spouse dies, see section 6013 and the related regulations.

(c) *Tax tables.* For rules on the use of the tax tables that apply to individuals, see section 3 and the related regulations.

(d) *Change in rates.* For the treatment of taxable years during which a change in the tax rates occurs, see section 15.

(e) *Applicability date.* This section applies to taxable years beginning after the date these regulations are published as final regulations in the **Federal Register**.

Par. 3. Section 1.2–2 is revised to read as follows:

### § 1.2–2 Definitions and special rules.

(a) *Surviving spouse*—(1) *In general.* If a taxpayer is eligible to file a joint return under section 6013 (without applying section 6013(a)(3)) for the taxable year in which the taxpayer's spouse dies, the taxpayer qualifies as a surviving spouse for each of the two taxable years immediately following the year of the spouse's death if the taxpayer—

(i) Has not remarried before the close of the taxable year; and

(ii) Maintains as the taxpayer's home a household that is for the taxable year the principal place of abode of a son or daughter (including by adoption), stepson, or stepdaughter who is a member of the taxpayer's household and who is a dependent of the taxpayer within the meaning of paragraph (a)(2) of this section.

(2) *Dependent*. An individual is a dependent of a taxpayer for purposes of this paragraph (a) if the taxpayer may claim a deduction under section 151 for the individual, without applying sections 152(b)(1), (b)(2), and (d)(1)(B).

(b) *Head of household*—(1) *In general*. A taxpayer qualifies as a head of household if the taxpayer is not married at the end of the taxable year, is not a surviving spouse, as defined in paragraph (a) of this section, and either—

(i) Maintains as the taxpayer's home a household that is for more than one-half of the taxable year the principal place of abode of a qualifying child or dependent of the taxpayer, within the meaning of paragraph (b)(2) of this section, who is a member of the taxpayer's household during that period; or

(ii) Maintains a household, whether or not the taxpayer's home, that is for the taxable year the principal place of abode of a parent of the taxpayer, within the meaning of paragraph (b)(3) of this section.

(2) *Qualifying child or dependent*—(i) *Qualifying child*. An individual is a qualifying child for purposes of this paragraph (b) if the individual is a qualifying child of the taxpayer as defined in section 152(c) and the related regulations, determined without applying section 152(e). However, if the individual is married at the end of the taxpayer's taxable year, the individual is not a qualifying child for purposes of this section if the individual is not the taxpayer's dependent because of the limitations of section 152(b)(2) (relating to an individual filing a joint return with his or her spouse) or 152(b)(3) (relating to individuals who are citizens or nationals of other countries).

(ii) *Dependent*. An individual is a dependent for purposes of this paragraph (b) if the individual is the taxpayer's dependent, within the meaning of section 152 without applying sections

152(d)(2)(H) (relating to an individual qualifying as a member of the household) and 152(d)(3) (relating to the special rule for multiple support agreements) for whom the taxpayer may claim a deduction under section 151.

(3) *Parent.* An individual is a parent of the taxpayer for purposes of this paragraph (b) if the individual is the taxpayer's father or mother, including a father or mother who legally adopted the taxpayer, and is the taxpayer's dependent within the meaning of section 152 without applying section 152(d)(3), relating to the special rule for multiple support agreements, for whom the taxpayer may claim a deduction under section 151.

(4) *Limitation.* An individual may qualify only one taxpayer as a head of household for taxable years beginning in the same calendar year.

(5) *Marital status.* For purposes of this paragraph (b), the marital status of a taxpayer is determined at the end of the taxpayer's taxable year. A taxpayer is considered not married if the taxpayer is legally separated from the taxpayer's spouse under a decree of divorce or separate maintenance, if at any time during the taxable year the taxpayer's spouse is a nonresident alien, or if the provisions of section 7703(b) are satisfied. A taxpayer is considered married if the taxpayer's spouse, other than a spouse who is a nonresident alien, dies during the taxable year.

(6) *Nonresident alien.* A taxpayer does not qualify as a head of household if the taxpayer is a nonresident alien, as defined in section 7701(b)(1)(B), at any time during the taxable year.

(c) *Member of the household.* An individual is a member of a taxpayer's household if the individual and the taxpayer reside in the same living quarters and the taxpayer maintains the household, in part, for the benefit of the individual. An individual is a member of a taxpayer's household despite a temporary absence due to special circumstances. An individual is not treated as a member of the taxpayer's household if, at any time during the taxable year of the taxpayer, the relationship between the individual and the taxpayer violates local law. See § 1.152–4(c)(2) for rules relating to temporary absences.

(d) *Maintaining a household*—(1) *In general.* A taxpayer maintains a household only if during the taxable year the taxpayer pays more than one-half of the cost of operating the household for the mutual benefit of the residents. These expenses include property taxes, mortgage interest, rent, utility charges, upkeep and repairs, property insurance, and food consumed on the premises. A taxpayer may treat a home's fair market rental value as a cost of maintaining a household, instead of the sum of payments for property taxes, mortgage interest, and property insurance. Expenses of maintaining a household do not include—

- (i) The cost of clothing, education, medical treatment, vacations, life insurance, and transportation;
- (ii) The value of services performed in the household by the taxpayer or any other person qualifying the taxpayer as a head of household or as a surviving spouse; or
- (iii) An expense paid or reimbursed by any other person.

(2) *Proration of costs.* In determining whether a taxpayer pays more than one-half of the cost of maintaining a household that is the principal place of abode of a qualifying child or dependent for less than a taxable year, the cost for the entire taxable year is prorated on the basis of the number of calendar months the qualifying child or dependent resides in the household. A period of less than a calendar month is treated as a full calendar month. Thus, for example, if the cost of

302

maintaining a household for a taxable year is $30,000, and a taxpayer shares a principal place of abode with a qualifying child or dependent from May 20 to December 31, the taxpayer must furnish more than $10,000 (8/12 of $30,000 × 50 percent) in maintaining the household from May 1 to December 31 to satisfy the requirements of this paragraph (d).

(3) *New household.* If a new household is established during the taxpayer's taxable year (for example, if spouses separate and one moves out of the family home with the child), the cost of maintaining the new household for the year is the cost of maintaining that household beginning with the date the new household is established. If one spouse and the child remain in the family home and the other parent moves out of the home, the cost of maintaining the household for the year is the cost of maintaining the household beginning with the date the other spouse moves out.

(4) *Birth, death, adoption, or placement.* If an individual is a member of a household for less than a taxable year as a result of the individual's birth, death, adoption, or placement with a taxpayer for adoption or in foster care during that year, the requirement that the individual be a member of the household for more than one-half of the taxable year is satisfied if the individual is a member of the household for more than one-half of the period after the individual's birth, adoption, or placement for adoption or in foster care or before the individual's death.

(5) *Shared residence*—(i) *In general.* If two or more taxpayers not filing a joint return reside in the same living quarters, each taxpayer may be treated as maintaining a separate household if each provides more than one-half of the cost of maintaining the separate household. For this purpose, two households in the same living quarters are not considered separate households if any individual in one household is the spouse of any individual in the other household, or if any individual in

one household may claim, or would have priority under the tiebreaker rules in section 152(c)(4) to claim, any individual in the other household as a dependent.

(ii) *Examples*. The following examples illustrate the rules in this paragraph (d)(5). In each example, assume that if a taxpayer may be treated as residing in a separate household, that taxpayer provides more than one-half of the cost of maintaining that household.

*Example 1*. Two sisters and their respective children reside in the same living quarters. Neither sister may claim the other sister as a dependent. Each sister pays more than one-half of the expenses for herself and her children, and each sister claims each of her own children as a dependent. Because neither sister may claim the other sister as a dependent, and because neither sister would have priority to claim any of the other sister's children as a qualifying child under the tiebreaker rules of section 152(c)(4), each sister is treated as maintaining a separate household.

*Example 2*. A and B, an unmarried couple, have two children together (C1 and C2) and all four individuals live in the same living quarters for the entire tax year. Both A and B contribute to paying the expenses of the couple and the two children. A has higher adjusted gross income than B. Each parent files a tax return. Under the tiebreaker rules in section 152(c)(4), the parent with the higher adjusted gross income (in this case, A) would have priority to claim each child as a qualifying child if both claimed the child. As a result, B may not be treated as maintaining a separate household with either child or both children. Therefore, if B may be claimed as A's dependent, then all four individuals are members of the same household. However, if B may not be claimed as A's dependent, B may be treated as maintaining a separate household consisting solely of B, even if B claims one of the children as a dependent on B's return.

*Example 3.* The facts are the same as in *Example 2* of this paragraph (d)(5)(ii) except that A and B do not have any children together; C1 is the child of A and C2 is the child of B. Neither A nor B may claim the other as a dependent, and each parent pays more than one-half of the expenses for himself or herself and his or her child. Because neither A nor B may claim the other adult or the other adult's child as a dependent, each adult is treated as maintaining a separate household.

*Example 4.* Grandparent, Parent, and Child live together and Child meets the definition of a qualifying child for both Parent and Grandparent. Both Parent and Grandparent pay their respective expenses, and both contribute to paying Child's expenses. Neither Parent nor Grandparent may claim the other as a dependent. Under the tiebreaker rules of section 152(c)(4), Parent would have priority over Grandparent to claim Child as a qualifying child. Therefore, Grandparent may not be treated as maintaining a household for Grandparent and Child separate from the household of Parent. However, Parent may be treated as maintaining a household for Parent and Child separate from the household of Grandparent.

(e) *Special rules for maintaining a household*—(1) *Principal place of abode.* For purposes of this section, the term *principal place of abode* has the same meaning as in section 152 and § 1.152–4(c).

(2) *Part-year residence.* If, during the taxable year, an individual who may qualify a taxpayer as head of household is born or dies, is adopted or lawfully placed for adoption with the taxpayer, is an eligible foster child, or is a missing child, whether the taxpayer maintained a household that is the principal place of abode of the individual for the required period is determined under § 1.152–4(d) and (e).

(3) *Change of location.* A taxpayer may maintain a household even though the physical location of the household changes.

(f) *Certain married individuals living apart.* An individual who is considered not married under section 7703(b) also is considered not married for all purposes of part I of subchapter A of chapter 1 of the Code.

(g) *Applicability date.* This section applies to taxable years beginning after the date these regulations are published as final regulations in the **Federal Register**.

Par. 4. Section 1.3–1 is revised to read as follows:

## § 1.3–1 Tax tables for individuals.

(a) *In general.* Except as otherwise provided in paragraph (b) of this section, in lieu of the tax imposed by section 1, an individual who does not itemize deductions for the taxable year and whose taxable income for the taxable year does not exceed the ceiling amount as defined in paragraph (c) of this section, must determine his or her tax liability under the prescribed tax tables in tax forms and publications of the Internal Revenue Service. The individual must use the appropriate tax rate category under the tax tables. The tax imposed under section 3 and this section shall be treated as tax imposed by section 1.

(b) *Exceptions.* Section 3 and this section do not apply to (1) an individual making a return for a period of fewer than 12 months as a result of a change in annual accounting period, or (2) an estate or trust.

(c) *Ceiling amount defined.* The ceiling amount means the highest amount of taxable income for which a tax amount is determined in the tax tables for the tax rate category in which the taxpayer falls.

(d) *Special rule for surviving spouse.* A taxpayer filing as a surviving spouse uses the same tax rate category as a taxpayer filing a joint return.

(e) *Applicability date.* This section applies to taxable years beginning after the date these regulations are published as final regulations in the **Federal Register**.

Par. 5. Section 1.21–1 is amended by revising paragraph (a)(1), removing paragraph (h), redesignating paragraphs (j), (k), and (l) as paragraphs (h), (j), and (k), and revising newly redesignated paragraph (k) to read as follows:

## § 1.21–1 Expenses for household and dependent care services necessary for gainful employment.

(a) *In general.* (1) Section 21 allows a credit to a taxpayer against the tax imposed by chapter 1 for employment-related expenses for household services and care (as defined in paragraph (d) of this section) of a qualifying individual (as defined in paragraph (b) of this section). The purpose of the expenses must be to enable the taxpayer to be gainfully employed (as defined in paragraph (c) of this section). For taxable years beginning after December 31, 2004, a qualifying individual must have the same principal place of abode (as defined by paragraph (g) of this section) as the taxpayer for more than one-half of the taxable year.

* * * * *

(k) *Applicability date*—(1) *In general.* Except as provide in paragraph (k)(2) of this section, this section and §§ 1.21–2 through 1.21–4 apply to taxable years ending after August 14, 2007.

(2) *Exception.* Paragraph (a)(1) of this section applies to taxable years beginning after the date these regulations are published as final regulations in the **Federal Register**.

Par. 6. Section 1.32–2 is amended by revising the section heading, adding paragraph (c)(3), and revising paragraph (e) to read as follows:

## § 1.32–2 Earned income credit.

\* \* \* \* \*

(c) \* \* \*

(3) *Qualifying child*—(i) *In general.* For purposes of this section, a qualifying child of the taxpayer is a qualifying child as defined in section 152(c), determined without applying sections 152(c)(1)(D) and 152(e).

(ii) *Application of tiebreaker rules.* For purposes of determining whether a taxpayer is an eligible individual under section 32(c)(1)(A), if an individual meets the definition of a qualifying child under paragraph (c)(3)(i) of this section for more than one taxpayer and the individual is treated as the qualifying child of a taxpayer under the tiebreaker rules of section 152(c)(4) and the related regulations, then that taxpayer may be an eligible individual under section 32(c)(1)(A)(i) and may claim the earned income credit for a taxpayer with a qualifying child if all other requirements of section 32 are satisfied. If an individual meets the definition of a qualifying child under paragraph (c)(3)(i) of this section for more than one taxpayer and the individual is not treated as the qualifying child of a taxpayer under the tiebreaker rules of section 152(c)(4) and the related regulations, then the individual also is not treated as a qualifying child of that taxpayer in the taxable year for purposes of section 32(c)(1)(A). Thus, that taxpayer may be an eligible individual under section 32(c)(1)(A)(ii) and may claim the earned income credit for a taxpayer without a qualifying child if all other requirements are satisfied.

(iii) *Examples*. The following examples illustrate the rules of this paragraph (c). In each example, the taxpayer uses the calendar year as the taxpayer's taxable year and, except to the extent indicated, each taxpayer meets the requirements to claim the benefits(s) described in the example.

*Example 1*. Child, Parent, and Grandparent share the same principal place of abode for the taxable year. Child meets the definition of a qualifying child under paragraph (c)(3)(i) of this section for both Parent and Grandparent (and for no other person) for the taxable year. Parent claims the earned income credit with Child as Parent's qualifying child. Under the tiebreaker rules of section 152(c)(4)(A) and the related regulations, Child is treated as the qualifying child of Parent and is not treated as the qualifying child of Grandparent. Under section 32(c)(1) and paragraph (c)(3)(ii) of this section, Parent is an eligible individual under section 32(c)(1)(A)(i) who may claim the earned income credit for a taxpayer with a qualifying child, and Grandparent is an eligible individual under section 32(c)(1)(A)(ii) who may claim the earned income credit for a taxpayer without a qualifying child.

*Example 2*. The facts are the same as in *Example 1* of this paragraph (c)(3)(iii), except that Grandparent, rather than Parent, claims Child as a qualifying child, and Grandparent's adjusted gross income is higher than Parent's adjusted gross income. Under the tiebreaker rules of section 152(c)(4)(C) and the related regulations, Child is treated as the qualifying child of Grandparent and is not treated as the qualifying child of Parent. Under section 32(c)(1) and paragraph (c)(3)(ii) of this section, Grandparent is an eligible individual under section 32(c)(1)(A)(i) who may claim the earned income credit for a taxpayer with a qualifying child, and Parent is an eligible individual under section 32(c)(1)(A)(ii) who may claim the earned income credit for a taxpayer without a qualifying child.

\* \* \* \* \*

(e) *Applicability date*—(1) *In general.* Except as provided in paragraph (e)(2) of this section, this section applies to taxable years beginning after March 5, 2003.

(2) *Exception.* Paragraph (c)(3) of this section applies to taxable years beginning after the date these regulations are published as final regulations in the **Federal Register**.

### § 1.63–1 [Amended]

Par. 7. Section 1.63–1 is amended by:

- 1. Removing the language "the zero bracket amount and" from the section heading.
- 2. Removing the language "section 63(g)" and replacing it with the language "section 63(e)" in paragraph (a).

Par. 8. Section 1.63–2 is revised to read as follows:

### § 1.63-2 Standard deduction

The standard deduction means the sum of the basic standard deduction and the additional standard deduction.

Par. 9. Section 1.63–3 is added to read as follows:

### § 1.63-3 Additional standard deduction for the aged and blind

(a) *In general.* A taxpayer who, at the end of the taxable year, has attained age 65 or is blind is entitled to an additional

310

standard deduction amount. The additional standard deduction amount is the sum of the amounts to which the taxpayer is entitled under paragraphs (b) and (c) of this section. If an individual meets the requirements for both the additional amount for the aged and the additional amount for the blind, the taxpayer is entitled to both additional amounts.

(b) *Additional amount for the aged*—(1) *Aged taxpayer or spouse*. A taxpayer is entitled to an additional amount under section 63(f)(1) if the taxpayer has attained age 65 before the end of the taxable year. If spouses file a joint return, each spouse who has attained age 65 before the end of the taxable year for which the spouses file the joint return is entitled to an additional amount. A married taxpayer who files a separate return is entitled to an additional amount for the taxpayer's spouse if the spouse has attained age 65 before the end of the taxable year and, for the calendar year in which the taxable year of the taxpayer begins, the spouse has no gross income and is not the dependent of another taxpayer. The taxpayer is not entitled to an additional amount if the spouse dies before attaining age 65, even though the spouse would have attained age 65 before the end of the taxpayer's taxable year.

(2) *Age determined*. For purposes of section 63(f) and this paragraph (b), a taxpayer's age is determined as of the last day of the taxpayer's taxable year. A person attains the age of 65 on the first moment of the day preceding his or her sixty-fifth birthday.

(c) *Additional amount for the blind*—(1) *Blind taxpayer or spouse*. A taxpayer is entitled to an additional amount under section 63(f)(2) if the taxpayer is blind at the end of the taxable year. If spouses file a joint return, each spouse who is blind at the end of the taxable year for which the spouses file the joint return is entitled to an additional amount. A married taxpayer who files a separate return is entitled to an additional amount for the taxpayer's spouse if the spouse is blind and, for the

311

calendar year in which the taxable year of the taxpayer begins, the spouse has no gross income and is not the dependent of another taxpayer. If the spouse dies during the taxable year, the date of death is the time for determining the spouse's blindness.

(2) *Blindness determined.* A taxpayer who claims an additional amount allowed by section 63(f)(2) for the blind must maintain in the taxpayer's records a statement from a physician skilled in the diseases of the eye or a registered optometrist stating that the physician or optometrist has examined the person for whom the additional amount is claimed and, in the opinion of the physician or optometrist, the person's central visual acuity did not exceed 20/200 in the better eye with correcting lenses, or the person's visual acuity was accompanied by a limitation in the field of vision such that the widest diameter of the visual field subtends an angle no greater than 20 degrees. The statement must provide that the physician or optometrist examined the person in the taxpayer's taxable year for which the amount is claimed, or that the physician or optometrist examined the person in an earlier year and that the visual impairment is irreversible.

(d) *Applicability date.* This section and §§ 1.63–1(a) and 1.63–2 apply to taxable years beginning after the date these regulations are published as final regulations in the **Federal Register**.

Par. 10. Section 1.151–1 is amended by revising paragraphs (a)(1), (c), and (d) to read as follows:

### Sec. 1.151-1 Deduction for personal exemptions

(a) * * * (1) In computing taxable income, an individual is allowed a deduction for the exemptions for an individual taxpayer and spouse (the personal exemptions) and the exemption for a dependent of the taxpayer.

\* \* \* \* \*

(c) *Additional exemption for dependent.* Section 151(c) allows a taxpayer an exemption for each individual who is a dependent (as defined in section 152) of the taxpayer for the taxable year. See §§ 1.152–1 through 1.152–5 for rules relating to dependents.

(d) *Applicability date.* Paragraphs (a)(1) and (c) of this section apply to taxable years beginning after the date these regulations are published as final regulations in the **Federal Register**.

## §§ 1.151–2, 1.151–3, and 1.151–4 [Removed]

Par. 11. Sections 1.151–2, 1.151–3, and 1.151–4 are removed.

Par. 12. Section 1.152–0 is added under the undesignated center heading Deductions for Personal Exemptions to read as follows:

## § 1.152–1 General rules for dependents.

(a) *In general*—(1) *Dependent defined.* Except as provided in section 152(b) and paragraph (a)(2) of this section, the term *dependent* means a qualifying child as described in § 1.152–2 or a qualifying relative as described in § 1.152–3. In general, an individual may be treated as the dependent of only one taxpayer for taxable years beginning in the same calendar year.

(2) *Exceptions*—(i) *Dependents ineligible.* If an individual is a dependent of a taxpayer for a taxable year of the taxpayer, the individual is treated as having no dependents for purposes of section 152 and the related regulations in the individual's taxable year beginning in the calendar year in which that taxable year of the taxpayer begins. For purposes of this paragraph (a)(2)(i), an individual is not a dependent of a

person if that person is not required to file an income tax return under section 6012 and either does not file an income tax return or files an income tax return solely to claim a refund of estimated or withheld taxes.

(ii) *Married dependents.* An individual is not treated as a dependent of a taxpayer for a taxable year of the taxpayer if the individual files a joint return, other than solely to claim a refund of estimated or withheld taxes, with the individual's spouse under section 6013 for the taxable year beginning in the calendar year in which that taxable year of the taxpayer begins.

(iii) *Citizens or nationals of other countries.* An individual who is not a citizen or national of the United States is not treated as a dependent of a taxpayer unless the individual is a resident, as defined in section 7701(b), of the United States or of a country contiguous to the United States (Canada or Mexico). This limitation, however, does not apply to an adopted child, as defined in section 152(f)(1)(B) and paragraph (b)(1)(ii) of this section, if the taxpayer is a citizen or national of the United States and the child has the same principal place of abode as the taxpayer and is a member of the taxpayer's household, within the meaning of §§ 1.152–4(c) and 1.2–2(c), respectively, for the taxpayer's taxable year. See § 1.152–4(d)(2) for rules relating to residence for a portion of a taxable year. A taxpayer and the child have the same principal place of abode for the taxpayer's taxable year if the taxpayer and child have the same principal place of abode for the entire portion of the taxable year following the placement of the child with the taxpayer.

(b) *Definitions.* The following definitions apply for purposes of section 152 and the related regulations.

(1) *Child*—(i) *In general.* The term *child* means a son, daughter, stepson, or stepdaughter, or an eligible foster child,

within the meaning of paragraph (b)(1)(iii) of this section, of the taxpayer.

(ii) *Adopted child*. In determining whether an individual bears any of the relationships described in paragraph (b)(1)(i) of this section, § 1.152–2(b), or § 1.152–3(b), a legally adopted child of a person, or a child who is lawfully placed with a person for legal adoption by that person, is treated as a child by blood of that person. A child lawfully placed with a person for legal adoption by that person includes a child placed for legal adoption by a parent, an authorized placement agency, or any other person(s) authorized by law to place a child for legal adoption.

(iii) *Eligible foster child*. The term *eligible foster child* means a child who is placed with a person by an authorized placement agency or by judgment, decree, or other order of any court of competent jurisdiction.

(iv) *Authorized placement agency*. The term *authorized placement agency* means a State, the District of Columbia, a possession of the United States, a foreign country, an Indian Tribal Government (ITG) (as defined in section 7701(a)(40)), or an agency or organization that is authorized by a State, the District of Columbia, a possession of the United States, a foreign country, an ITG, or a political subdivision of any of the foregoing, to place children for legal adoption or in foster care.

(2) *Student*. The term *student* means an individual who, for some part of each of five calendar months, whether or not consecutive, during the calendar year in which the taxable year of the taxpayer begins, either is a full-time student at an educational organization, as defined in section 170(b)(1)(A)(ii), or is pursuing a full-time course of institutional on-farm training under the supervision of an accredited agent of an educational organization or of a State or political subdivision of a State. A full-time student is one who

is enrolled for the number of hours or courses that the educational organization considers full-time attendance.

(3) *Brother and sister*. The terms *brother* and *sister* include a brother or sister by half blood.

(4) *Parent*. The term *parent* refers to a biological or adoptive parent of an individual. It does not include a stepparent who has not adopted the individual.

(c) *Applicability date*. This section, and §§ 1.152–2, 1.152–3, and 1.152–4 apply to taxable years beginning after the date these regulations are published as final regulations in the **Federal Register**.

Par. 14. Section 1.152–2 is revised to read as follows:

**§ 1.152–2 Qualifying child.**

(a) *In general*. The term *qualifying child* of a taxpayer for a taxable year means an individual who satisfies the tests described in paragraphs (b), (c), (d), (e), and (f) of this section. If an individual satisfies the definition of a qualifying child for more than one taxpayer, then the tiebreaker rules in paragraph (g) of this section apply. See, however, section 152(e) and § 1.152–5 for a special rule for a child of divorced or separated parents or parents who live apart.

(b) *Qualifying child relationship test*. The individual must bear one of the following relationships to the taxpayer—

- (1) A child of the taxpayer or descendant of such a child; or
- (2) A brother, sister, stepbrother, or stepsister of the taxpayer, or a descendant of any of these relatives.

(c) *Residency test.* The individual must have the same principal place of abode as the taxpayer for more than one-half of the taxable year. Generally, an individual has the same principal place of abode as the taxpayer for more than one-half of the taxable year if the individual resides with the taxpayer for more than one-half of the taxable year. See § 1.152–4(c) for rules relating to principal place of abode and temporary absence and for determining whether an individual resides with the taxpayer for more than one-half of the taxable year.

(d) *Age test*—(1) *In general.* The individual must be younger than the taxpayer claiming the individual as a qualifying child and must not have attained the age of 19, or age 24 if the individual is a student within the meaning of § 1.152–1(b)(2), as of the end of the calendar year in which the taxpayer's taxable year begins. For purposes of this section, an individual attains an age on the anniversary of the individual's birth.

(2) *Disabled individual.* This age requirement is treated as satisfied if the individual is permanently and totally disabled, as defined in section 22(e)(3), at any time during the calendar year.

(e) *Qualifying child support test.* The individual must not provide more than one-half of the individual's own support for the calendar year in which the taxpayer's taxable year begins. See § 1.152–4(a) for rules relating to the definition and sources of an individual's support.

(f) *Joint return test.* The individual must not file a joint return, other than solely to claim a refund of estimated or withheld taxes, under section 6013 with the individual's spouse for the taxable year beginning in the calendar year in which the taxpayer's taxable year begins.

(g) *Child who is eligible to be claimed as a qualifying child by more than one taxpayer*—(1) *In general.* Under section

152(c)(4), if an individual satisfies the definition of a qualifying child for two or more taxpayers (eligible taxpayers) for a taxable year beginning in the same calendar year, the following rules apply.

(i) *More than one eligible parent.* If more than one eligible taxpayer is a parent of the individual (eligible parent), any one of the eligible parents may claim the individual as a qualifying child. However, if more than one eligible parent claims the individual as a qualifying child, and those eligible parents do not file a joint return with each other, the individual is treated as the qualifying child of the eligible parent claiming the individual with whom the individual resides for the longest period of time during the taxable year as determined under § 1.152–4(c)(3). If the individual resides for the same amount of time during the taxable year with each eligible parent claiming the child, the individual is treated as the qualifying child of the eligible parent with the highest adjusted gross income who claims the individual.

(ii) *Eligible parent not claiming.* If at least one eligible taxpayer is a parent of the individual, but no eligible parent claims the individual as a qualifying child, the individual may be treated as the qualifying child of another eligible taxpayer only if that taxpayer's adjusted gross income exceeds both the adjusted gross income of each eligible parent of the individual and the adjusted gross income of each other eligible taxpayer, if any.

(iii) *One eligible parent and other eligible taxpayer(s).* Except as provided in paragraph (g)(1)(i) or (ii) of this section, if there are two or more eligible taxpayers, only one of whom is the parent of the individual, the individual is treated as the qualifying child of the eligible parent.

(iv) *No eligible parent.* If no eligible taxpayer is a parent of the individual, the individual is treated as the qualifying child of the eligible taxpayer with the highest adjusted gross income for the taxable year.

(2) *Determination of adjusted gross income of a person who files a joint return.* For purposes of section 152 and the related regulations, the adjusted gross income of each person who files a joint return is the total adjusted gross income shown on the joint return.

(3) *Coordination with other provisions.* Except to the extent that section 152(e) and § 1.152–5 apply, if more than one taxpayer may claim a child as a qualifying child, the child is treated as the qualifying child of only one taxpayer for purposes of head of household filing status under section 2(b), the child and dependent care credit under section 21, the child tax credit under section 24, the earned income credit under section 32, the exclusion from income for dependent care assistance under section 129, and the dependency exemption under section 151. Thus, the taxpayer claiming the individual as a qualifying child under any one of these sections is the only taxpayer who may claim any credit or exemption under these other sections for that same individual for a taxable year beginning in the same calendar year as the taxpayer's taxable year. If section 152(e) applies, however, the noncustodial parent may claim the child as a qualifying child for purposes of the dependency exemption and the child tax credit, and another person may claim the child for purposes of one or more of these other provisions. See § 1.152–5 for rules under section 152(e).

(4) *Examples.* The following examples illustrate the rules in this paragraph (g). In the examples, each taxpayer uses the calendar year as the taxpayer's taxable year, the child is a qualifying child (as described in section 152(c) and this section) of each taxpayer, and, except to the extent indicated, each taxpayer meets the requirements to claim the benefit(s) described in the example.

*Example 1.* (i) A and B, parents of Child, are married to each other. A, B, and Child share the same principal place of abode for the first 8 months of the year. Thus, both parents satisfy the qualifying child residency test of paragraph (c) of this section. For the last 4 months of the year, the parents live apart from each other, and B and Child share the same principal place of abode. Section 152(e), relating to divorced or separated parents, does not apply. The parents file as married filing separately for the taxable year, and both parents claim Child as a qualifying child.

(ii) Under paragraph (g)(1)(i) of this section, Child is treated as a qualifying child of B for all purposes, because Child resided with B for the longer period of time during the taxable year. Because section 152(e) does not apply, Child may not be treated as a qualifying child of A for any purpose.

*Example 2.* (i) The facts are the same as in *Example 1* of this paragraph (g)(4), except that B does not claim Child as a qualifying child.

(ii) Because A and B are not both claiming the same child as a qualifying child, under paragraph (g)(1)(i) of this section, Child is treated as a qualifying child of A.

*Example 3.* (i) Child, Child's parent (D), and Grandparent share the same principal place of abode. D is not married and is not a qualifying child or dependent of Grandparent, and Grandparent is not D's dependent. Section 152(e), relating to divorced or separated parents, does not apply. Under paragraph (a) of this section, Child meets the definition of a qualifying child of both D and Grandparent. D claims Child as a qualifying child for purposes of the child and dependent care credit under section 21, the earned income credit under section 32, and the dependency exemption under section 151. Grandparent claims Child as a qualifying child for purposes of head of household filing status under section 2(b).

(ii) Under paragraph (g)(1)(iii) of this section, Child is treated as the qualifying child of D for all purposes, because D is eligible to claim and claims Child as D's qualifying child. Because D is eligible to claim and claims Child as D's qualifying child, under paragraph (g)(3) of this section, Child may not be treated as a qualifying child of Grandparent for any purpose. Grandparent erroneously claimed Child as Grandparent's qualifying child for purposes of head of household filing status under section 2(b). If D had not claimed Child as D's qualifying child for any purpose, under paragraph (g)(1)(ii) of this section, Grandparent could have claimed Child as Grandparent's qualifying child if Grandparent's adjusted gross income (AGI) exceeded D's AGI. In that situation, under paragraph (g)(3) of this section, Grandparent could have claimed Child as Grandparent's qualifying child for purposes of any of the child-related tax benefits, provided that Grandparent had met the requirements of those sections.

*Example 4.* (i) The facts are the same as in *Example 3* of this paragraph (g)(4), except that Child's parents, D and E, are married to each other and share the same principal place of abode with Child and Grandparent for the entire taxable year. Under paragraph (a) of this section, Child meets the definition of a qualifying child of both parents and Grandparent. D and E file a joint return for the taxable year and do not claim Child as a qualifying child for any purpose.

(ii) Because D or E may claim Child as a qualifying child but neither claims Child as a qualifying child for any purpose, under paragraph (g)(1)(ii) of this section, Grandparent may claim Child as a qualifying child if Grandparent's AGI exceeds the total AGI reported on the joint return of D and E.

*Example 5.* (i) The facts are the same as in *Example 4* of this paragraph (g)(4), except that D and E are divorced from each other, E moved into a separate residence during that year and is the noncustodial parent, and section 152(e), relating to divorced or separated parents, applies. E attaches to E's return a Form 8332 on which D agrees to release D's claim to a dependency exemption for Child and E claims Child as a qualifying child for purposes of the dependency exemption and the child tax credit.

(ii) Under paragraph (g)(3) of this section, Child is treated as a qualifying child of E for purposes of the dependency exemption and the child tax credit. Child may be treated as a qualifying child of D for purposes of the earned income credit. If D claims Child as a qualifying child for purposes of the earned income credit, under paragraph (g)(1)(iii) of this section, Child may not be treated as a qualifying child of Grandparent for any purpose.

*Example 6.* (i) F and G, parents of two children, are married to each other. F, G, and both children share the same principal place of abode for the entire taxable year. F and G file as married filing separately for the taxable year. F claims the older child as a qualifying child for purposes of the child tax credit, dependency exemption, and the child and dependent care credit. G claims the younger child as a qualifying child for purposes of the same three tax benefits.

(ii) The older child is treated as a qualifying child of F and the younger child is treated as a qualifying child of G. The tiebreaker rule of paragraph (g)(1)(i) of this section does not apply because F and G are not claiming the same child as a qualifying child.

Par. 15. Section 1.152–3 is revised to read as follows:

## § 1.152–3 Qualifying relative.

(a) *In general.* The term *qualifying relative* of a taxpayer for a taxable year means an individual who satisfies the tests described in paragraphs (b), (c), (d), and (e) of this section.

See, however, section 152(e) and § 1.152–5 for a special rule for a child of divorced or separated parents or parents who live apart.

(b) *Qualifying relative relationship test.* The individual must bear one of the following relationships to the taxpayer:

- (1) A child or descendant of a child;
- (2) A brother, sister, stepbrother, or stepsister;
- (3) A father or mother, or an ancestor of either;
- (4) A stepfather or stepmother;
- (5) A niece or nephew;
- (6) An aunt or uncle;
- (7) A son-in-law, daughter-in-law, father-in-law, mother-in-law, brother-in-law, or sister-in-law; or
- (8) An individual (other than one who at any time during the taxable year was the taxpayer's spouse, determined without regard to section 7703) who for the taxable year of the taxpayer has the same principal place of abode as the taxpayer and is a member of the taxpayer's household. See § 1.2–2(c) for the definition of a member of the household, and § 1.152–4(c) for rules relating to the meaning of principal place of abode and the meaning of temporary absence.

(c) *Gross income test*—(1) *In general.* The individual's gross income for the calendar year in which the taxable year begins must be less than the exemption amount as defined in section 151(d).

(2) *Income of disabled or handicapped individuals.* For purposes of paragraph (c)(1) of this section, the gross income of an individual who is permanently and totally disabled, as defined in section 22(e)(3), at any time during the taxable year does not include income for services performed by the individual at a sheltered workshop, as defined in section 152(d)(4)(B), if—

- (i) The principal reason for the individual's presence at the workshop is the availability of medical care there; and
- (ii) The individual's income arises solely from activities at the workshop that are incident to the medical care.

(d) *Qualifying relative support test*—(1) *In general.* The individual must receive over one-half of the individual's support from the taxpayer for the calendar year in which the taxpayer's taxable year begins. See § 1.152–4(a) for rules relating to support.

(2) *Certain income of taxpayer's spouse.* A payment to a spouse that is includible in the payee spouse's gross income under section 71 (relating to alimony and separate maintenance payments) or section 682 (relating to income of an estate or trust in the case of divorce) is not treated as a payment by the payor spouse for the support of any dependent.

(3) *Support from stepparent.* Any support provided to or for the benefit of an individual by a stepparent of the individual is treated as support provided by the individual's parent who is married to the stepparent.

(4) *Multiple support agreements.* If more than one-half of an individual's support is provided by two or more persons together, a taxpayer is treated as having contributed over one-half of the support of that individual for the calendar year if—

- (i) No one person contributes more than one-half of the individual's support;
- (ii) Each member of the group that collectively contributes more than one-half of the support of the individual would have been entitled to claim the individual as a dependent for a taxable year beginning in that calendar year but for the fact that the group

member alone did not contribute more than one-half of the individual's support;

- (iii) The taxpayer claiming the individual as a qualifying relative contributes more than 10 percent of the individual's support; and
- (iv) Each other group member who contributes more than 10 percent of the support of the individual furnishes to the taxpayer claiming the individual as a dependent a written declaration that the other person will not claim the individual as a dependent for any taxable year beginning in that calendar year.

(e) *Not a qualifying child test*—(1) *In general.* The individual must not be a qualifying child of the taxpayer or of any other taxpayer for any taxable year beginning in the calendar year in which the taxpayer's taxable year begins. An individual is not a qualifying child of a person, however, if that person is not required to file an income tax return under section 6012, and either does not file an income tax return or files an income tax return solely to claim a refund of estimated or withheld taxes.

(2) *Examples.* The following examples illustrate the rules in this paragraph (e). In each example, each taxpayer uses the calendar year as the taxpayer's taxable year, and except to the extent otherwise indicated, each taxpayer meets the requirements to claim the benefits described in the example.

*Example 1.* For the taxable year, B provides more than one-half of the support of an unrelated friend, C, and C's 3-year-old child, D, who are members of B's household. No taxpayer other than C is eligible to claim D as a qualifying child. C has no gross income, is not required by section 6012 to file a Federal income tax return, and does not file a Federal income tax return for the taxable year. Under paragraph (e)(1) of this section, because C does not have a filing requirement and does not file an income tax return, D is not treated as a qualifying child of C, and B may claim both C and D as B's qualifying relatives.

*Example 2.* The facts are the same as in *Example 1* of this paragraph (e)(2) except that C has earned income of $1,500 during the taxable year, had income tax withheld from C's wages, and is not required by section 6012 to file an income tax return. C files an income tax return solely to obtain a refund of withheld taxes and does not claim the earned income credit under section 32. Under paragraph (e)(1) of this section, because C does not have a filing requirement and files only to obtain a refund of withheld taxes, D is not treated as a qualifying child of C, and B may claim both C and D as B's qualifying relatives.

*Example 3.* The facts are the same as in *Example 2* of this paragraph (e)(2) except that C's earned income is more than the amount of the dependency exemption for that year. C files an income tax return for the taxable year to obtain a refund of withheld taxes and claims the earned income credit. Because C filed an income tax return to obtain the earned income credit and not solely to obtain a refund of withheld taxes, D is a qualifying child of a taxpayer (C), and B may not claim D as a qualifying relative. B also may not claim C as a qualifying relative because C fails the gross income test under paragraph (c) of this section.

Par. 16. Redesignate § 1.152–4 as § 1.152–5, and add a new § 1.152–4 to read as follows:

## § 1.152–4 Rules for a qualifying child and a qualifying relative.

(a) *Support*—(1) *In general.* The term *support* includes food, shelter, clothing, medical and dental care, education, and similar items. Support does not include an individual's Federal, State, and local income taxes paid from the individual's own income or assets, Social Security and Medicare taxes under section 3101 paid from the individual's own income, life insurance premiums, or funeral expenses. In determining whether an individual provided more than one-half of the individual's own support for purposes of § 1.152–2(e), or whether a taxpayer provided more than one-half of an individual's support for purposes of § 1.152–3(d), the amount of support provided by the individual, or the taxpayer, is compared to the total amount of the individual's support from all sources. For these purposes, except as otherwise provided in this paragraph (a), the amount of an individual's total support is the amount of support from all sources, and includes support the individual provides and amounts that are excludable from gross income. Generally, the amount of an item of support is the amount of expense paid or incurred to furnish the item of support. If the item of support furnished is property or a benefit, such as lodging, however, the amount of the item of support is the fair market value of the item.

(2) *Payments made during the year for unpaid or future support.* For purposes of determining the amount of support provided in a calendar year, an amount paid in a calendar year after the calendar year in which the liability is incurred is treated as paid in the year of payment. An amount paid in a calendar year before due, whether or not made in the form of a lump sum payment in settlement of a person's liability for support, is treated as support paid during the calendar year of payment rather than the calendar year when payment is due. A payment of a liability from amounts set aside in trust in a prior year is treated as made in the year in which the liability is paid.

(3) *Governmental payments*—(i) *Governmental payments as support*—(A) *In general.* Except as provided in paragraph (a)(3)(iii) of this section, governmental payments and subsidies for an item of support are support provided by a third party, the government.

(B) *Examples*. Payments of Temporary Assistance for Needy Families (42 U.S.C. 601–619), low-income housing assistance (42 U.S.C. 1437f), Supplemental Nutrition Assistance Program benefits (7 U.S.C. chapter 51), Supplemental Security Income payments (42 U.S.C. 1381–1383f), foster care maintenance payments, and adoption assistance payments are governmental payments and subsidies for an item of support as described in paragraph (a)(3)(i)(A) of this section.

(ii) *Governmental payments based on a taxpayer's contributions*—(A) *In general*. Except as provided in paragraph (a)(3)(iii) of this section, governmental payments based on a taxpayer's earnings and contributions into the Social Security system are support provided by the individual for whose benefit the payments are made to the extent those payments are used for that individual's support.

(B) *Examples*. Social Security old age benefits under section 202(b) of Title II of the Social Security Act (SSA) (42 U.S.C. 402) are governmental payments based on a taxpayer's earnings and contributions into the Social Security system as described in paragraph (a)(3)(ii)(A) of this section. Similarly, Social Security survivor and disability insurance benefits paid under section 202(d) of the SSA to, or for the benefit of, the child of a deceased or disabled parent are treated as support provided by the child to the extent those payments are used for the child's support.

(iii) *Payments used for support of another individual*. Governmental payments and subsidies described in paragraph (a)(3)(i) of this section and governmental payments described in paragraph (a)(3)(ii) of this section that are used by the recipient or other intended beneficiary to support another person are support of that person provided by the recipient or other intended beneficiary, rather than support provided by a third party, the government.

(4) *Medical insurance.* Medical insurance premiums, including Part A Basic Medicare premiums, if any, under Title XVIII of the Social Security Act (42 U.S.C. 1395c to 1395i–5), Part B Supplemental Medicare premiums under Title XVIII of the Social Security Act (42 U.S.C. 1395j to 1395w–6), Part C Medicare + Choice Program premiums under Title XVIII of the Social Security Act (42 U.S.C. 1395w–21 to 1395w–29), and Part D Voluntary Prescription Drug Benefit Medicare premiums under Title XVIII of the Social Security Act (42 U.S.C. 1395w–101 to 1395w–154), are treated as support. Medical insurance proceeds, including benefits received under Medicare Part A, Part B, Part C, and Part D, are not treated as items of support and are disregarded in determining the amount of the individual's support. Services provided to an individual under the medical and dental care provisions of the Armed Forces Act (10 U.S.C. chapter 55) are not treated as support and are disregarded in determining the amount of the individual's support.

(5) *Medical care payments from personal injury claim.* Payments for the medical care of an injured individual from a third party, including a third party's insurance company, in satisfaction of a legal claim for the personal injury of the individual are not treated as items of support and are disregarded in determining the amount of the individual's support.

(6) *Scholarships.* Amounts a student who is the child of the taxpayer receives as a scholarship for study at an educational organization described in section 170(b)(1)(A)(ii) are not treated as an item of support and are disregarded in determining the amount of the student's support.

(b) *Relationship test*—(1) *Joint return.* A taxpayer may satisfy the relationship test described in § 1.152–2(b) (relating to a qualifying child) or in § 1.152–3(b) (relating to a qualifying relative) if a described relationship exists between an individual and the taxpayer claiming that individual as a qualifying child or qualifying relative, even though the taxpayer files a joint return with his or her spouse who does not have a described relationship with the individual.

(2) *Divorce or death of spouse.* If the relationship between the taxpayer and an individual claimed by that taxpayer as a dependent results from a marriage, the taxpayer's qualifying relationship with the individual continues after the termination of the marriage by divorce or death.

(c) *Principal place of abode*—(1) *In general.* The term *principal place of abode* of a person means the primary or main home or dwelling where the person resides. A person's principal place of abode need not be the same physical location throughout the taxable year and may be temporary lodging such as a homeless shelter or relief housing resulting from displacement caused by a natural disaster.

(2) *Temporary absence.* The taxpayer and an individual have the same principal place of abode despite a temporary absence by either person because of special circumstances. An absence is temporary if the person would have resided at the place of abode but for the absence and, under the facts and circumstances, it is reasonable to assume that the person will return to reside at the place of abode. An individual who does not reside with the taxpayer because of a temporary absence is treated as residing with the taxpayer. For example, a nonpermanent failure to occupy the abode by reason of illness, education, business, vacation, military service, institutionalized care for a child who is totally and permanently disabled (as defined in section 22(e)(3)), or incarceration may be treated as a temporary absence because of special circumstances. If an infant must remain in a hospital for a period of time after birth and would have resided with the taxpayer during that period but for the hospitalization, the

infant is treated as having the same principal place of abode as the taxpayer during the period of hospitalization.

(3) *Residing with taxpayer for more than one-half of the taxable year*—(i) *In general.* An individual has the same principal place of abode as the taxpayer for more than one-half of the taxable year if the individual resides with the taxpayer for at least 183 nights during the taxpayer's taxable year, or 184 nights if the taxable year includes a leap day.

(ii) *Nights of residence*—(A) *Nights counted.* For purposes of determining whether an individual resides with the taxpayer for more than one-half of the taxable year, an individual resides with a taxpayer for a night if the individual sleeps—

- (*1*) At the taxpayer's principal place of abode, whether or not the taxpayer is present; or
- (*2*) In the company of the taxpayer when the individual does not sleep at the taxpayer's principal place of abode (for example, when the taxpayer and the individual are on vacation).

(B) *Night straddling two taxable years.* If an individual resides with a taxpayer for a night that extends over two taxable years, that night is allocated to the taxable year in which the night begins.

(C) *Exception for a parent who works at night.* If, in a calendar year, because of a taxpayer's nighttime work schedule, an individual resides for at least 183 days, or 184 days if the taxable year includes a leap day, but not nights with the taxpayer, the individual is treated as residing with the taxpayer for more than one-half of the taxable year.

(D) *Absences.* An individual who does not reside with a taxpayer for a night because of a temporary absence as described in paragraph (c)(2) of this section is treated as residing with the taxpayer for that night if the individual would have resided with the taxpayer for that night but for the absence.

(4) *Examples*. The following examples illustrate the rules of this paragraph (c). In each example, each taxpayer uses the calendar taxable year, and section 152(e) does not apply.

*Example 1*. B and C are the divorced parents of Child. In 2015, Child sleeps at B's principal place of abode for 210 nights and at C's principal place of abode for 155 nights. Under paragraph (c)(3) of this section, Child resides with B for at least 183 nights during 2015 and has the same principal place of abode as B for more than one-half of 2015.

*Example 2*. D and E are the divorced parents of Child, and Grandparent is E's parent. In 2015, Child resides with D for 140 nights, with E for 135 nights, and with Grandparent for the last 90 nights of the year. None of these periods is a temporary absence. Under paragraph (c)(3) of this section, Child does not have the same principal place of abode as D, E, or Grandparent for more than one-half of 2015.

*Example 3*. The facts are the same as in *Example 2* of this paragraph (c)(4), except that, for the 90-day period that Child lives with Grandparent, E is temporarily absent on military service. Child would have lived with E if E had not been absent during that period. Under paragraphs (c)(2) and (c)(3)(ii)(D) of this section, Child is treated as residing with E for 225 nights in 2015 and, therefore, Child has the same principal place of abode as E for more than one-half of 2015.

*Example 4*. The facts are the same as in *Example 2* of this paragraph (c)(4), except that, for the last 90 days of the year Child, who is 18, moves into Child's own apartment and begins full-time employment. Because Child's absence is not temporary, under paragraph (c)(2) of this section, Child is not treated as residing with D or E for the 90 nights. Under paragraph (c) of this section, Child does not have the same principal place of abode as D or E for more than one-half of 2015.

*Example 5.* F and G are the divorced parents of Child. In 2015, Child sleeps at F's principal place of abode for 170 nights and at G's principal place of abode for 170 nights. Child spends 25 nights of the year away from F and G at a summer camp. Child would have spent those nights with F if Child had not gone to summer camp. Under paragraphs (c)(2) and (c)(3)(ii)(D) of this section, Child is treated as residing with F for 195 nights and, therefore, Child has the same principal place of abode as F for more than one-half of 2015.

*Example 6.* H and J are the divorced parents of Child. In 2015, Child sleeps at H's principal place of abode for 180 nights and at J's principal place of abode for 180 nights. For 5 nights during that year, Child sleeps at Grandparent's abode or at the house of a friend. Child would have spent all 5 nights at H's house if Child had not slept at Grandparent's or a friend's house. Under paragraphs (c)(2) and (c)(3)(ii)(D) of this section, Child is treated as residing with H for 185 nights and, therefore, Child has the same principal place of abode as H for more than one-half of 2015.

(d) *Residence for a portion of a taxable year because of special circumstances*—(1) *Individual who is born or dies during the year.* If an individual is born or dies during a taxpayer's taxable year, the residency test for a qualifying child is treated as met if the taxpayer and the individual have the same principal place of abode for more than one-half of the portion of the taxable year during which the individual is alive. If an individual is born or dies during a taxpayer's taxable year, the relationship test for a qualifying relative who is a member of the taxpayer's household is treated as met if the taxpayer and the individual have the same principal place of abode for the entire portion of the taxable year during which the individual is alive.

(2) *Adopted child or foster child.* If, during a taxpayer's taxable year, the taxpayer adopts a child, a child is lawfully placed with a taxpayer for legal adoption by that taxpayer, or an eligible foster child is placed with a taxpayer, the residency test for a qualifying child and the residency requirement under § 1.152–1(a)(2)(iii) for a child who is not a citizen or national of the United States are treated as met if the taxpayer and the child have the same principal place of abode for more than one-half of the portion of the taxable year as required for a qualifying child, or for the entire taxable year as required for a noncitizen, following the placement of the child with the taxpayer.

(e) *Missing child*—(1) *Qualifying child.* A child of the taxpayer who is presumed by law enforcement authorities to have been kidnapped by someone who is not a member of the family of either the child or the taxpayer, and who had for the taxable year in which the kidnapping occurred the same principal place of abode as the taxpayer for more than one-half of the portion of the taxable year before the date of the kidnapping, is treated as meeting the residency test for a qualifying child, as described in § 1.152–2(c), of the taxpayer for all taxable years ending during the period that the child is missing. Also, the child is treated as meeting the residency test in the year of the child's return if the child has the same principal place of abode as the taxpayer for more than one-half of the portion of the taxable year following the date of the child's return.

(2) *Qualifying relative.* A child of the taxpayer who is presumed by law enforcement authorities to have been kidnapped by someone who is not a member of the family of either the child or the taxpayer, and who was a qualifying relative of the taxpayer for the portion of the taxable year

before the date of the kidnapping, is treated as a qualifying relative, as described in section 152(d) and § 1.152–3, of the taxpayer for all taxable years ending during the period that the child is missing. Also, the child is treated as a qualifying relative of the taxpayer in the year of the child's return if the child is a qualifying relative of the taxpayer for the portion of the taxable year following the date of the child's return.

(3) *Age limitation.* The special rules provided in this paragraph (e) cease to apply as of the first taxable year of the taxpayer beginning after the calendar year in which there is a determination that the child is dead or, if earlier, in which the child would have attained age 18.

(4) *Application.* This paragraph (e) applies solely for purposes of determining surviving spouse or head of household filing status under section 2, the child tax credit under section 24, the earned income credit under section 32, and the dependency exemption under section 151.

Par.17 In newly redesignated § 1.152–5, paragraphs (e)(2), (e)(3)(iii), and (h) are revised to read as follows:

### § 1.152–5 Special rule for a child of divorced or separated parents or parents who live apart.

\* \* \* \* \*

(e)

(2) *Attachment to return*—(i) *In general.* A noncustodial parent must attach a copy of the written declaration to the parent's original or amended return for each taxable year for which the noncustodial parent claims an exemption for the child. A noncustodial parent may submit a copy of the written declaration to the IRS during an examination to substantiate a claim to a dependency exemption for a child. A copy of a

written declaration attached to an amended return, or provided during an examination, will not meet the requirement of this paragraph (e) if the custodial parent signed the written declaration after the custodial parent filed a return claiming a dependency exemption for the child for the year at issue, and the custodial parent has not filed an amended return to remove that claim to a dependency exemption for the child.

(ii) *Examples*. The following examples illustrate the rules of this paragraph (e).

*Example 1*. Custodial parent (CP) files her 2015 return on March 1, 2016, and claims a dependency exemption for Child. At noncustodial parent's (NCP) request, CP signs a Form 8332 for the 2015 tax year on April 15, 2016. On April 15, NCP files his return claiming a dependency exemption for Child and attaches the signed Form 8332 to his return. Under section 152(e) and paragraph (b) of this section, NCP is allowed a dependency exemption for Child for 2015, and CP is not allowed a dependency exemption for Child for that year.

*Example 2*. The facts are the same as in *Example 1* of this paragraph (e)(2)(ii), except NCP files on April 15, 2016, a request for an extension to file his tax return because he does not have a signed Form 8332. CP signs the Form 8332 for the 2015 tax year in August of 2016, and NCP files his return a week later. NCP claims a dependency exemption for Child and attaches the signed Form 8332 to his return. Under section 152(e) and paragraph (b) of this section, NCP is allowed a dependency exemption for Child for 2015, and CP is not allowed a dependency exemption for Child for that year.

*Example 3*. CP files his 2015 return on March 1, 2016, and claims a dependency exemption for Child. NCP files her return on April 15, 2016, and does not claim a dependency exemption for Child, even though her divorce decree allocates the dependency exemption for Child to her. CP signs a Form 8332 for the 2015 tax year in August of 2016, and NCP files an amended return a week later and attaches the signed Form 8332 to her amended return claiming a dependency exemption for Child. Under paragraph (e)(2) of this section, NCP is not allowed a dependency exemption for Child for 2015 if CP has not amended his return to remove a claim to the dependency exemption for Child for that year.

(3) * * *

(iii) *Attachment to return.* The parent revoking the written declaration must attach a copy of the revocation to the parent's original or amended return for each taxable year for which the parent claims a child as a dependent as a result of the revocation. The parent revoking the written declaration must keep a copy of the revocation and evidence of delivery of the notice to the other parent, or of the reasonable efforts to provide actual notice. A parent may submit a copy of a revocation to the IRS during an examination to substantiate a claim to a dependency exemption for the child.

* * * * *

(h) *Applicability date*—(1) *In general.* Except as provided in paragraph (h)(2) of this section, this section applies to taxable years beginning after July 2, 2008.

(2) *Exception.* Paragraphs (e)(2) and (e)(3)(iii) of this section apply to taxable years beginning after the date these regulations are published as final regulations in the **Federal Register**.

## § 1.6013–1 [Amended]

Par. 18. Section 1.6013–1 is amended by removing paragraph (e).

## PART 301—PROCEDURE AND ADMINISTRATION

Par. 19. The authority citation for part 301 continues to read in part as follows:

Authority: 26 U.S.C. 7805 * * *

Par. 20. Section 301.6109–3 is amended by:

- 1. Revising the first sentence and adding a sentence to the end of the paragraph in paragraph (a)(1).
- 2. Revising paragraphs (b), (c)(1)(ii), the fourth and fifth sentences of (c)(2) introductory text, and paragraph (d).

The revisions and addition read as follows:

### § 301.6109–3 IRS adoption taxpayer identification numbers.

(a) *In general*—(1) *Definition.* An IRS adoption taxpayer identification number (ATIN) is a temporary taxpayer identifying number assigned by the Internal Revenue Service (IRS) to a child (other than an alien individual as defined in § 301.6109–1(d)(3)(i)) who has been placed lawfully with a prospective adoptive parent for legal adoption by that person. * * * A child lawfully placed with a prospective adoptive parent for legal adoption includes a child placed for legal adoption by the child's parent or parents by blood, an authorized placement agency, or any other person authorized by State law to place a child for legal adoption.

* * * * *

(b) *Definitions*—(1) Authorized placement agency has the same meaning as in § 1.152–1(b)(1)(iv).

(2) *Child* means a child who has not been adopted but has been placed lawfully with a prospective adoptive parent for legal adoption by that person.

(3) *Prospective adoptive parent* means a person in whose household a child has been placed lawfully for legal adoption by that person.

(c) * * *

(1) * * *

(ii) The child has been placed lawfully with the prospective adoptive parent for legal adoption by that person;

* * * * *

(2) * * * In addition, the application must include documentary evidence the IRS prescribes to establish that a child has been placed lawfully with the prospective adoptive parent for legal adoption by that person. Examples of acceptable documentary evidence establishing lawful placement for a legal adoption may include—

* * * * *

(d) *Applicability date*—(1) *In general*. Except as otherwise provided in paragraph (d)(2) of this section, the provisions of this section apply to income tax returns due (without regard to extension) on or after April 15, 1998.

(2) *Exception*. Paragraphs (a)(1), (b), (c)(1)(ii), and (c)(2) of this section apply to income tax returns due (without regard to extension) on or after the date these regulations are published as final regulations in the **Federal Register**.

*John Dalrymple Deputy Commissioner for Services and Enforcement.*

## Note

(Filed by the Office of the Federal Register on January 18, 2017, 8:45 a.m., and published in the issue of the Federal Register for January 19, 2017, 82 F.R. 6370.)

--------------------------

## Definition of Terms and Abbreviations

## Definition of Terms

*Revenue rulings and revenue procedures (hereinafter referred to as "rulings") that have an effect on previous rulings use the following defined terms to describe the effect:*

*Amplified* describes a situation where no change is being made in a prior published position, but the prior position is being extended to apply to a variation of the fact situation set forth therein. Thus, if an earlier ruling held that a principle applied to A, and the new ruling holds that the same principle also applies to B, the earlier ruling is amplified. (Compare with *modified,* below).

*Clarified* is used in those instances where the language in a prior ruling is being made clear because the language has caused, or may cause, some confusion. It is not used where a position in a prior ruling is being changed.

*Distinguished* describes a situation where a ruling mentions a previously published ruling and points out an essential difference between them.

*Modified* is used where the substance of a previously published position is being changed. Thus, if a prior ruling held that a principle applied to A but not to B, and the new ruling holds that it applies to both A and B, the prior ruling is modified because it corrects a published position. (Compare with *amplified* and *clarified*, above).

*Obsoleted* describes a previously published ruling that is not considered determinative with respect to future transactions. This term is most commonly used in a ruling that lists previously published rulings that are obsoleted because of changes in laws or regulations. A ruling may also be obsoleted because the substance has been included in regulations subsequently adopted.

*Revoked* describes situations where the position in the previously published ruling is not correct and the correct position is being stated in a new ruling.

*Superseded* describes a situation where the new ruling does nothing more than restate the substance and situation of a previously published ruling (or rulings). Thus, the term is used to republish under the 1986 Code and regulations the same position published under the 1939 Code and regulations. The term is also used when it is desired to republish in a single ruling a series of situations, names, etc., that were previously published over a period of time in separate rulings. If the new ruling does more than restate the substance of a prior ruling, a combination of terms is used. For example, *modified* and *superseded* describes a situation where the substance of a previously published ruling is being changed in part and is continued without change in part and it is desired to restate the valid portion of the previously published ruling in a new ruling that is self contained. In this case, the previously published ruling is first modified and then, as modified, is superseded.

*Supplemented* is used in situations in which a list, such as a list of the names of countries, is published in a ruling and that list is expanded by adding further names in subsequent rulings. After the original ruling has been supplemented several times, a new ruling may be published that includes the list in the original ruling and the additions, and supersedes all prior rulings in the series.

*Suspended* is used in rare situations to show that the previous published rulings will not be applied pending some future action such as the issuance of new or amended regulations, the outcome of cases in litigation, or the outcome of a Service study.

## Abbreviations

*The following abbreviations in current use and formerly used will appear in material published in the Bulletin.*

*A*—Individual.

*Acq.*—Acquiescence.

*B*—Individual.

*BE*—Beneficiary.

*BK*—Bank.

*B.T.A.*—Board of Tax Appeals.

*C*—Individual.

*C.B.*—Cumulative Bulletin.

*CFR*—Code of Federal Regulations.

*CI*—City.

*COOP*—Cooperative.

*Ct.D.*—Court Decision.

*CY*—County.

*D*—Decedent.

*DC*—Dummy Corporation.

*DE*—Donee.

*Del. Order*—Delegation Order.

*DISC*—Domestic International Sales Corporation.

*DR*—Donor.

*E*—Estate.

*EE*—Employee.

*E.O.*—Executive Order.

*ER*—Employer.

*ERISA*—Employee Retirement Income Security Act.

*EX*—Executor.

*F*—Fiduciary.

*FC*—Foreign Country.

*FICA*—Federal Insurance Contributions Act.

*FISC*—Foreign International Sales Company.

*FPH*—Foreign Personal Holding Company.

*F.R.*—Federal Register.

*FUTA*—Federal Unemployment Tax Act.

*FX*—Foreign corporation.

*G.C.M.*—Chief Counsel's Memorandum.

*GE*—Grantee.

*GP*—General Partner.

*GR*—Grantor.

*IC*—Insurance Company.

*I.R.B.*—Internal Revenue Bulletin.

*LE*—Lessee.

*LP*—Limited Partner.

*LR*—Lessor.

*M*—Minor.

*Nonacq.*—Nonacquiescence.

*O*—Organization.

*P*—Parent Corporation.

*PHC*—Personal Holding Company.

*PO*—Possession of the U.S.

*PR*—Partner.

*PRS*—Partnership.

*PTE*—Prohibited Transaction Exemption.

*Pub. L.*—Public Law.

*REIT*—Real Estate Investment Trust.

*Rev. Proc.*—Revenue Procedure.

*Rev. Rul.*—Revenue Ruling.

*S*—Subsidiary.

*S.P.R.*—Statement of Procedural Rules.

*Stat.*—Statutes at Large.

*T*—Target Corporation.

*T.C.*—Tax Court.

*T.D.*—Treasury Decision.

*TFE*—Transferee.

*TFR*—Transferor.

*T.I.R.*—Technical Information Release.

*TP*—Taxpayer.

*TR*—Trust.

*TT*—Trustee.

*U.S.C.*—United States Code.

*X*—Corporation.

*Y*—Corporation.

*Z*—Corporation.

# Index

Notes

Notes

www.ingramcontent.com/pod-product-compliance
Lightning Source LLC
Chambersburg PA
CBHW021028210326
41598CB00016B/943